BIBLE
Nobodies
WHO
BECAME
Somebodies

BIBLE
Nobodies
WHO
BECAME
Somebodies

LANCE WUBBELS
& TERRY McDOWELL

Literary development and cover/interior design by Koechel Peterson & Associates, Inc. Minneapolis, Minnesota.

Destiny Image® Publishers, Inc.
P.O. Box 310
Shippensburg, PA 17257-0310
"Speaking to the Purposes of God for This Generation
and for the Generations to Come"

ISBN 0-7684-3022-4

For Worldwide Distribution
Printed in the U.S.A.

Manufactured in the United States of America.

This book and all other Destiny Image,
Revival Press, MercyPlace, Fresh Bread, Destiny Image Fiction,
and Treasure House books are available
at Christian bookstores and distributors worldwide.

1 2 3 4 5 6 7 8 9 10 / 09 08 07 06 05 04

For a U.S. bookstore nearest you, call
1-800-722-6774.

For more information on foreign distributors, call
717-532-3040.

Or reach us on the Internet: **www.destinyimage.com**

COMPILERS

L ANCE WUBBELS is presently the Vice President of Literary Development at Koechel Peterson & Associates, Inc. For the previous eighteen years, Wubbels worked as the Managing Editor of Bethany House Publishers as well as a teacher at Bethany College of Missions in Bloomington, Minnesota.

He is the author of the recently released *A Time for Heroes* with Destiny Image, *If Only I Knew* with Hallmark Books, and *A Woman in the Making* with J. Countryman®. He has published seven fiction books with Bethany House Publishers and won an Angel Award for his novel, *One Small Miracle*. He has also compiled and edited twenty-five Christian Living Classic books published by Emerald Books. His daily devotional, *In His Presence*, won the 1999 Gold Medallion Award from the Evangelical Christian Publishers Association.

Wubbels was assisted in this project by TERRY MCDOWELL, who provided a great deal of research and development for these readings. McDowell is a veteran editor/literary developer, who worked as an editor first with Editorial Betania and later with Bethany House Publishers. He is presently the Editorial Director for Nelson Reference, a division of Thomas Nelson, Inc.

Compiled and Adapted refers to the fact that Wubbels and McDowell searched for these short chapters through the classic writings of numerous legendary Christian expositors from the nineteenth century, which they have adapted and rewritten for today's reader. Charles Spurgeon, Joseph Parker, Alexander Whyte, Alexander Maclaren, James Hastings, and others provided their ageless messages that were totally renewed to become as relevant today as the day they were penned.

CONTENTS

· · · · · · · · · · · · ● ● ● · · · · · · · · · · · · · ·

INTRODUCTION

I N A TWENTY-FIRST CENTURY WORLD that seems to be
spinning out of control faster and faster, a frightening shadow
has fallen over people's lives that only intensifies the serious
life challenges they are already facing. God has provided His people with His inspired Word as an anchor of stability for these troubled times, and as a compass to guide them through the dense
forests of confusing philosophies and the swamps of changing
ethics. The Bible is filled with countless examples of those who
chose to live their lives in faith and obedience to God despite the
overwhelming odds they faced or the tempting opportunities to
compromise their beliefs.

Many of the biblical characters we often read about were powerful leaders and heroes, such as Moses, Elisha, Daniel, the great
apostle Paul, and John on the island of Patmos. But others, often
overlooked by us, lived their lives in what some would call the
obscure shadowlands of insignificance—Barzillai, Ahithophel,
Hadad, Hoglah, and Lydia. They are the lesser known people we
find tucked here and there in the pages of sacred Scripture. Several
of them are never even given names, such as the Shunammite
woman or the Syrophenician woman or the little boy who gave
Jesus his loaves and fishes to feed a starving multitude. You've
probably never even heard of some of them before. But it is important to realize that the telling of their stories, too, was inspired by
God and included for a reason—all the way from Genesis to
Revelation—so that we can glean meaningful lessons for our lives.

You will find that God used people from all walks of life, not
just the biblical superstars we are most familiar with. The moments
of destiny in the lives of these ordinary people will rekindle a spark
of hope for that same destiny for your life today. The eyes of our
heavenly Father are upon the lives of every person who yields to

Him, no matter how insignificant that person may appear to be in the total scheme of history. Through our humble faith and obedience, God takes our ordinary lives and uses them for the working of His extraordinary eternal plan for this world, whether or not they are perceived as important or valuable.

No one disputes the validity of studying the great discourses given by Moses, Solomon, or Jesus Himself as fountains of divine wisdom. But we often miss pearls of great truth in the stories of biblical people we have rarely heard of. In our reading of the Scriptures, have we relegated them to the realm of irrelevance, deemed them to be nobodies? God spoke of them intentionally, and though we might consider them Bible *nobodies*, they truly became *somebodies*.

It should be noted that these short chapters were compiled and significantly adapted or rewritten for today's reader from the classic writings of numerous legendary Christian expositors. Charles Spurgeon, Joseph Parker, Alexander Whyte, James Hastings, Alexander Maclaren, and others provided their ageless messages that were totally renewed to become as relevant today as the day they were penned. We hope you'll open your heart to the Spirit of God as you read and discover afresh His wisdom to guide you through life.

ABIGAIL

The Nobody Whose Husband Was a Fool

Now Samuel died, and all Israel assembled and mourned for him;
and they buried him at his home in Ramah. Then David moved down
into the Desert of Maon. A certain man in Maon, who had property
there at Carmel, was very wealthy. He had a thousand goats
and three thousand sheep, which he was shearing in Carmel.
His name was Nabal and his wife's name was Abigail.
She was an intelligent and beautiful woman, but her husband,
a Calebite, was surly and mean in his dealings.

1 SAMUEL 25:1-3

. . . . ● ● ● ● ● . . . .

THE STORY OF ABIGAIL owes part of its charm to its unexpectedness. It is a marvel to find a woman of such excellence married to a man so vulgar and rude as Nabal. He is the ultimate jerk who treats everyone as though he owns them, the creep who is so easy to despise.

It seems likely, given Abigail's grace and worth, that her marriage had been arranged by their parents and not by Abigail's choice. Nabal was a descendent of the noble family of Caleb, and he was a man of considerable wealth. Family and property were powerful factors in the marriage market back then and often overlooked a thousand shortcomings, of which Nabal had an abundance. Money talked just as loudly then as it does now.

David had come to take part in the nation's lament at Ramah for the death of the prophet Samuel, who had been both David's master and friend. David did not, however, dare to trust himself in such close proximity to King Saul. As soon as the burial was over, David returned to the sparsely populated region of Paran, at the extreme south of Judah. His military presence in these borderlands had brought tranquillity and safety to the inhabitants there.

At the time of David's sojourn in this district, Nabal held his annual sheep shearing. This event was equivalent to the harvest of the flock masters and was commonly finished with a joyous feast. It was a season of liberality and goodwill. In the present situation, David knew that Nabal had specific reasons for being satisfied with the returns from his shepherds, for David and his men had been the literal guardians of Nabal's property. It was a tacit understanding, an unwritten law, that David and his men should be rewarded during this time of celebration.

But when David sent messengers to remind Nabal of his obligations, all they received was a full blast of the surly man's meanness. "Who is this David? Who is this son of Jesse?" (1 Samuel 25:10) It was such a wicked reproach that when David heard it, he was so angered that he ordered four hundred of his men to arm themselves and follow him, vowing to not leave a single male survivor in the house of Nabal. Thus David was about to break the peace of the land, to seize the possessions of strangers, and to stain himself with the blood of peaceful citizens. Nabal's insolence, as horribly offensive as it was, did not justify death for himself or for any of his people. David would have appeared before God and all the world as an outlaw and certainly would have been considered unworthy of the crown of Israel.

However, one of the servants who heard Nabal hurl his insults told Abigail what happened, and how "night and day [David and his men] were a wall around us all the time we were herding our sheep near them" (v. 16). This servant trusted the wisdom of Abigail, though he considered her husband "such a wicked man that no one can talk to him" (v. 17). The servant's appeal was not in vain, for Abigail quickly loaded stores of supplies on donkeys and personally met David as he and his men approached. With remarkable tact and intelligence, she fell at David's feet and knew exactly what to say and how to say it to get past David's anger and into his heart.

One might have thought that the prospect of Nabal's death at David's hands would have been welcomed by Abigail, especially when his insolence invited it. But revenge was not her way. She was loyal to her husband, despite the fact that he deserved nothing. Though it might be impossible for Abigail to love him or respect him, Nabal is her husband, and she will do whatever she can within her power to stand between him and his foolishness. She does not dismiss his dreadful conduct, but she can truthfully tell David that Nabal is a fool by nature and not worthy of his regard. She goes so far as to say, "My lord, let the blame be on me alone" (v. 24).

David's eyes, still burning with wrath, rest upon this woman so fair, and he carefully considers her words. What can his response be but to be overwhelmed? His anger subsides, and Nabal and his people are spared. Abigail even congratulates David, telling him that the Lord has withheld him from shedding blood, touching upon his conscience and turning his gratitude to her into thanksgiving to God (vv. 32-34). It is hard to tell a man he is doing wrong, especially when he is full of anger, much less keep him from taking offense, but that is exactly what Abigail did. She is a remarkable woman of the highest virtue.

Abigail also placed before David a high ideal for the future. By her promises of the rich blessings with which the Lord would give to David, she gave such clear and distinct expression to her firm belief in the divine election of David as king of Israel that her words almost amounted to prophecy. "For the LORD will certainly make a lasting dynasty for my master, because he fights the LORD's battles" (v. 28). Then followed the well-known words, full of deep meaning and bursting with hope for the future: "The life of my master will be bound securely in the bundle of the living by the LORD your God" (v. 29). The metaphor is taken from the custom of binding up valuable things in a bundle to prevent them from being injured. The reference here is to the safe preservation of the righteous on this earth in the gracious fellowship of the Lord in this life, so that no enemy can harm him.

There was power in Abigail's argument, but what evidently touched David the most was her reference to his being the object of God's love and care. To be restrained by a loving God, to be in favor with Him amid the wrongs of evil men, to have an interest in the higher spiritual life that is nourished and guarded by the grace of God, was overwhelming to David. How could one so richly and undeservedly blessed be revengeful or act in any way unworthy of the name of God?

While we blame David for his heedless passion, we must not less admire the readiness with which he listened to Abigail's reasonable counsel. He recognized the hand of God and divine mercy in Abigail's coming, and he gave thanks. "Praise be to the LORD, the God of Israel, who has sent you today to meet me. May you be blessed for your good judgment and for keeping me from bloodshed this day and from avenging myself with my own hands" (vv. 32-33). It is a mark of sincere and genuine godliness to be not less thankful for being kept from sinning than for being rescued from suffering for that sin.

Remarkably, David is soon given a convincing proof that it is best to leave vengeance in God's hands. When the drunken Nabal sobers up and hears Abigail's story of direct intervention, he appears to suffer a stroke and then ten days later: "The LORD struck Nabal and he died" (vv. 37-38).

When David heard of the fate of Nabal, he sent his servants to bring Abigail to him to be his wife. It is obvious how deeply Abigail's wisdom and beauty had won his heart. Abigail, recognizing in this new incident of her life the guidance of a higher Hand, arose and went to him.

LIFE LESSON

· · · · · · · · · · · · · · · · · ● ● ● ● ● · · · · · · · · · · · · · · · · ·

We should never underestimate God's ability to intervene and bring justice to light despite the darkness around us. Injustice is always repaid, and evil still works together for the good of those who love the Lord (Romans 8:28). Sooner or later the Nabals of this world receive their just reward, even without requiring the Davids to become their own avengers. Thus God brings light out of darkness, a higher step of virtue out of what would have been a sin, and order out of confusion. This is the masterpiece of His wisdom, that, without preventing evil by force, He leaves men relatively free, but not the less incessantly keeps back the sinner on his perverted way, and weaves our unconstrained action as a thread in the web of His scheme of the universe. Only God can perform such wonders!

JAMES HASTINGS

AENEAS

The Nobody Who Got a Real Tune-Up for His Body

*As Peter traveled about the country, he went to visit the saints in
Lydda. There he found a man named Aeneas, a paralytic who had
been bedridden for eight years. "Aeneas," Peter said to him,
"Jesus Christ heals you. Get up and take care of your mat."
Immediately Aeneas got up. All those who lived in Lydda
and Sharon saw him and turned to the Lord.*

ACTS 9:32-35

JESUS HAD RISEN FROM THE DEAD, and Pentecost had
come, baptizing the disciples in the Holy Spirit. In obedience to the command Jesus had given at His ascension, Peter
was traveling through the country and preaching the good news
of the gospel. On this occasion, he came to visit the saints who
were in Lydda, a town northwest of Jerusalem and near Joppa,
which was on the Mediterranean coast. During his visit, Peter
came across a man with the classic name of Aeneas—no "mighty
warrior," however—but a poor paralyzed man who had been confined to the relative obscurity of his bed for eight long years. He
was a nobody's nobody, whom God was looking upon as a some-
body worthy of His powerful touch.

Moved by the sight of the man's crippling feebleness, Peter felt
the impulse of the Holy Spirit upon him. Looking at Aeneas as he
lay there, Peter said, "Aeneas, Jesus Christ heals you. Get up and
take care of your mat." Touched by the same Spirit who had inspired
the apostle, Aeneas believed that Christ had healed him and immediately rose up and made his bed. And in that instant his health was
perfectly restored. Talk about getting the people's attention in that

city. The news of what happened spread like wildfire, and Peter had an instant audience!

The text clearly indicates that Aeneas had been very sick for a long time. Imagine his friends seeing him, year after year, lying completely paralyzed in his bed, which had grown hard as a stone beneath him. This man's sickness was no figment of his imagination. He could not move, for the paralysis had completely immobilized him.

But paralysis is not limited just to our physical body. It also can affect our mind and our spirit. Are you paralyzed like Aeneas, but in a spiritual sense? Has the Spirit of God made you realize that you can do nothing right apart from Him, and that you are totally ruined and paralyzed unless Jesus Christ saves you? If so, do not despair because of how terrible your soul feels. His conviction is His gracious invitation. On the contrary, say to yourself, "There is room for mercy in me." Be encouraged with the hope that God will make the infirmity of your body or the paralysis of your soul an opportunity to display His mighty power. Remember, "I am the LORD, the God of all mankind. Is anything too hard for me?" (Jeremiah 32:27)

Aeneas had been paralyzed for *eight years*. The length of its endurance is a terrible element in any disease. And it was a disease that was *entirely incurable then*. Aeneas could not restore himself, and no mere human physician had the necessary skill to do anything for him either. Has the Spirit of God made you feel that your soul's wound is incurable? There is no soul physician except at Calvary; no healing but in the Savior's bleeding wounds.

Aeneas must have known something about Jesus, because, otherwise, when Peter said, "Get up and take care of your mat," Aeneas would have asked Peter what he meant. Aeneas could not intelligently have acted on what he could not comprehend. He could not have believed what Peter said, because he would not have understood his meaning. Mere words, unless they appeal to the understanding, cannot be useful. They must first open our eyes to see something from a new perspective, or they cannot inspire faith. When Peter said, "Aeneas, Jesus Christ heals you," no doubt Aeneas remembered what he had already heard about Jesus Christ. Peter was only watering the seed of faith that had already taken root in Aeneas's heart.

Aeneas had heard of these great miracles. The story of God taking on human form in Jesus had reached his ears by some means. Something of the wonder he had heard of this Nazarene who had healed the blind, cleansed lepers, and set people free from demons began to stir inside him. He understood that though Jesus Christ was no longer on earth but ascended to heaven, and there was only Peter and a few friends here, yet Jesus' power on earth was the same as it ever was. He believed that Jesus could work miracles from heaven as well as when He walked here on earth. Aeneas believed that He who healed the paralytics when He was here could heal the paralytics now that He had risen to His throne. And so Aeneas believed in Jesus Christ from what he had heard, simply trusting in Him for healing. By means of that faith Aeneas was made whole.

Aeneas did not believe in Peter as the healer, for you notice Peter did not say anything about himself. Peter preached too clear of a gospel for that. The purest gospel is that which has the least of man in it, and the most of God. Aeneas had no faith in any supposed power coming from Peter, and much less had he any faith in himself. Neither did he look within himself for any hope. By his faith he showed that it was not mere speculation, but solid practical believing.

And what exactly did Aeneas believe? He believed—and may you believe the same!—first, that Jesus could heal *him, Aeneas.* He simply believed that Jesus Christ could heal him without any preparation, just as he was, then, immediately, with a present salvation that would make him completely whole. When you think of who Christ is, and what He has done, it ought not be too difficult to believe in His miraculous healing power. But God's power must

21

be revealed before your soul will believe this salvation for your body, soul, and spirit. Yet it is true that Jesus Christ can heal, and can heal at once.

Whatever the sin is, He can cure that too. The scarlet fever of pride, the loathsome leprosy of lust, the shivering tremors of unbelief, the paralysis of greed—He can heal them all, and with a word, instantaneously, forever, completely, right now. David learned this and penned words of hope for every sinner who has fallen into believing the lie that he or she cannot be cleansed: "Cleanse me with hyssop, and I will be clean; wash me, and I will be whiter than snow" (Psalm 51:7).

But do not think that we speak about the pardon of past sin only. Pardon of sin, without deliverance from its power, would be a curse rather than a blessing. But wherever sin is pardoned, God also breaks the bondage of its power over the soul. If you are a slave to sins, Jesus can give perfect freedom from enslaving habits. If those sins coil about your heart and poison your life like serpents writhing within your conscience, Jesus can take them out of your soul and deliver you from the deadly effects of their fiery venom.

When Aeneas was healed, he acted according to the truth of that healing. When Peter told him to get up and make his bed, he rose immediately and obeyed. This man who had been paralyzed for eight years proved he was healed by making his bed. Here was a common man whose simple faith and obedience brought the good news of salvation closer to the hearts of all those around him. The Scripture says that all those who lived in Lydda and Sharon saw what had happened to him and turned to the Lord. Just think of the widespread effect his healing had. It opened the eyes of others to who Jesus really was and brought spiritual healing to many. That is the marvelous bounty of the Lord's grace. It ever extends to touch and heal all those who will believe by faith.

LIFE LESSON

· · · · · · · · · · · · · · · · · ● ● ● ● · · · · · · · · · · · · · · · · ·

D o not let the power of the sin that plagues you hold you back from coming to Jesus. The apostle Paul encourages us to have faith in the power of grace: "But where sin increased, grace increased all the more, so that, just as sin reigned in death, so also grace might reign through righteousness" (Romans 5:20). Jesus Christ did not come into the world to save pretend sinners but real sinners. Neither did He descend from heaven to seek those who are not diseased with sin, for those who are healthy and have no need of a physician. He has come to seek those who are deeply diseased and to give them real healing in your body as well as your soul. Jesus Christ will not forgive your past sin and then leave you to live the same life as before. Whatever the sin is that is now a disease to your soul, Jesus Christ can heal you of it. Believe and rise up healed!

CHARLES SPURGEON

AHITHOPHEL

The Nobody Who Thought David Was His Friend

Now in those days the advice Ahithophel gave
was like that of one who inquires of God.
That was how both David and Absalom regarded all
of Ahithophel's advice.

2 SAMUEL 16:23

. . . . ● ● ● . . . .

AHITHOPHEL WAS FAR AND AWAY the ablest and the most famous politician in the days of David, although we seldom notice or hear from him. The counsel of Ahithophel was a proverb in Israel at that time, but as often as we read the account, he appears to be an insignificant name that is easily passed over. The only one comparable to Ahithophel in his day was Hushai the Arkite, another of David's astutest counselors.

If the traditional interpretations of Psalm 55 and some other Ahithophel psalms are true, David and Ahithophel had been good friends since childhood. Ahithophel may not have been exactly a Jonathan to David, yet he appears to have been a very dear and well-deserving friend. It is believed that Ahithophel is the person referred to when David wrote these words: "But it is you, a man like myself, my companion, my close friend, with whom I once enjoyed sweet fellowship as we walked with the throng at the house of God" (Psalm 55:13-14). From the time that David was elevated to the throne of Israel and through all the best and most shining years of David's kingdom, Ahithophel was proud to lay all his magnificent gifts of sound advice and incomparable counsel at David's disposal. These were the good times for both David and Ahithophel, which unfortunately did not last.

As committed as Ahithophel was to David in matters of the state, so Ahithophel's only son, Eliam, was as devoted to David in the army and the field of battle. Now, Eliam had a daughter at home, Bathsheba, a beautiful young woman, who fell in love with and married Uriah, one of the captains of the mighty men. So it was that Ahithophel, Eliam, and Uriah served David, and David's power increased until the king of Israel denied himself nothing on which he set his heart. And in an evil hour David set his eyes and heart on Bathsheba, who was Ahithophel's only grandchild.

It does not take an oracle of God to tell us how Ahithophel felt about the ruin of his grandchild and the murder of her husband at David's hands. That Ahithophel and Eliam would remain in David's service while Bathsheba shared David's bed and her husband was in his grave is absurd.

After Ahithophel had left David, God sent Nathan to David to deliver His condemnation for David's sins. David is warned that from within his own house the sword would arise, which played itself out with a dreadful vengeance that tore the house of David to shreds (2 Samuel 12). Eventually, David's son Absalom stole the hearts of the men of Israel, and he called for Ahithophel to become his counselor. With bitter malice in his heart and the brilliant counsel of Ahithophel, Absalom forged a strong conspiracy to overthrow his father. Had not David been crafty enough to send Hushai the Arkite to deceive Absalom and counteract the counsels of Ahithophel (2 Samuel 15:32-37), Absalom would have prevailed. As it was, when Ahithophel saw that his counsel had not been followed by Absalom in favor of Hushai, he departed to his home, put his affairs in order, and hanged himself at Giloh (2 Samuel 17:23).

Ahithophel has been called a traitor, deserter, apostate, suicide, and all manner of evil names because he left David and joined Absalom. I would not be so harsh. Put yourself in his place for a moment and consider how deeply Ahithophel had suffered because of David's sins. David, his longtime friend, had betrayed that friendship and shattered his family and his career. Is there anything more agonizing to the soul than the faithlessness of a friend? My purpose is neither to whitewash Ahithophel nor blacken David, but to let you see yourself in them both as in a mirror. How, then, have you always acted toward those of your former friends who have injured you and your family? Ahithophel should have found a way to forgive David and not align himself with Absalom, but he did not. And often we have not forgiven as well.

I believe also that David took it upon himself that he was the reason Ahithophel had gone over to Absalom's side. David knew all the time whose grandchild Uriah's wife was. David knew as well as all Jerusalem did what it was that had driven Ahithophel to cross the line. Every time he thought of Ahithophel he must have said to himself, "I did it. He is there today because of the evil I have done." And, then, what did David think when Ahithophel's terrible end was told him? And what did Bathsheba think? Did she fling David's psalms in his face in her agony of horror and self-disgust? Did she scream in her sleep till all Jerusalem heard her as she saw in her nightmares her grandfather's gallows at Giloh?

And then did David go out to Giloh, and over the sepulchre of the suicide did he fall down and cry, "O Ahithophel, the friend of my youth and my best counselor! Would God that I had died in your place?"

LIFE LESSON

· · · · · · · · · · · · · · · · · · ● ● ● · · · · · · · · · · · · · · · · · · ·

Sin in our lives can have a profound effect upon the lives of those around us, especially those who are close to us. In David's case, the lust and the lies and the murder were devastating upon his family, friends, and a whole nation. Our own neglect of duty, our laziness and procrastination, our indiscretions of speech, our anger, and our foolish immorality can do the same. If you have people whom you have hurt and offended, ask the living God to help you go and make it all up to them. Do not put it off. Go and ask forgiveness and make restitution wherever possible. Don't wait for your situation to get worse as David did.

ALEXANDER WHYTE

AZARIAH

The Nobody Who Couldn't Wait for Pentecost

The Spirit of God came upon Azariah son of Oded.

2 CHRONICLES 15:1

. . . . ● ● ● ● ● ● . . . .

S UCH WORDS SHOULD DELIGHT US as well as grip our hearts. Here is the eternal Spirit of God, and here is the individual man upon whom the Holy Spirit has suddenly and graciously come upon in power. If you read the entire chapter, you discover all that we know about Azariah, the son of Oded, who became a remarkable prophet in the days of King Asa, who ruled Judah, the southern kingdom, about thirty years after King David. Through the words Azariah spoke, this Bible nobody stirred up the king and the people to seek the Lord with all their hearts. They heeded the prophet's words, and a great reformation transformed the entire nation.

Though thousands of years have transpired, God is still here, and man is still here. Why should divine encounters of this sort cease, as some would have us believe? Men and women still depend upon the living God for instruction, truth, inspiration, and guidance, and they are still made in the image and likeness of God. Nothing has changed concerning our need for revelation, the illumination of the mind, the preparation of the heart, and the sudden creation of light in the midst of the clouds and storms of life. Why should He withhold from us the living air of the Holy Spirit, which, breathing through our souls, purifies and elevates every faculty of our being? There is no reason why God should stop working this way. There is, on the other hand, every reason why it should continue and abound.

Asserting that the Spirit of God works directly upon human hearts, as He did in Azariah's life, certainly opens the door to potential false claims, dangers, and abuses. But the proposition is not the less true because the abuses are many and serious. Man can pervert anything. He would corrupt the heavens and extinguish all the stars if his wicked fingers could reach them. We are not, therefore, to be alarmed by the suggestion of danger and perversion when we state the true principle of the ongoing intervention of the divine in human lives.

The Spirit of God coming upon our lives is the greatest event in the human experience. We call it conversion, which is the finest word in anyone's life. There is no mistaking when it happens. When a man is converted to Jesus Christ, all things become new through the Holy Spirit (2 Corinthians 5:17). The heavens are so much higher, yet so much nearer; the earth is so much lovelier and more useful for spiritual ends. Our whole relationship to one another also is dramatically changed: we are enabled to love even our enemies and to pray for those who despitefully use and persecute us (Matthew 5:44). It is as though the whole sky of human experience suddenly lights up by the Spirit's indwelling of our lives—every faculty expands, burns, and becomes eager for action; all proportions are altered instantly; great things become small; insignificant things are charged with great meanings; time dies like a bubble in the air; and nothing is so present to the imagination and the whole consciousness as eternity.

Inspired men such as Azariah are blessed with the great gift of prophetic authority. The words he speaks do not die on his lips and do not come with apologies. The truths he utters do not ask for consideration but seem to step down from above and bring their own credentials with them. The inspired man is fearless. Asa the king is nothing to Azariah, because he has been with the living God. Azariah is a prophet who knows the presence of God; therefore, the king is a common man. The prophet knows where he stands, and the words he speaks are measured and powerful. That power expresses itself in perfect ease. He is calm and in no hurry; he is masterful, because he is wise; he has lived and moved and had his being in God, so what can man do to him?

Some people are only qualified by education, which is the poorest of all qualifications. To be able to speak ten languages and repeat others' philosophies may make us cultured, yet leave us unqualified. Education labors and discovers by long processes, and then announces in halting terms what it has discovered. Divine inspiration flies straight down from heaven and affirms itself with all the frankness of honesty and all the holy positiveness of personal experience. Inspiration, you see, is the life that has been bathed in heaven, expending itself upon earth in the encouraging, directing, healing, and uplifting of mankind.

Azariah had a clear message to deliver. He went to meet King Asa and said to him, "Listen to me, Asa and all Judah and Benjamin. The LORD is with you when you are with him. If you seek him, he will be found by you, but if you forsake him, he will forsake you" (2 Chronicles 15:2). This is the eternal plan: God and man in relationship. No other law is possible. There is nothing dogmatic or arbitrary about this declaration. We may deafen ourselves to it, turn away from it and fill our ears with other voices and create a pagan Pentecost of our own, but there comes a time, one quiet, solemn hour, when we must face it. This is the divine starting point. We cannot run into the darkness and enjoy the sunlight. No man can take the sun with him into the darkness: the terms are contradictory, the relations are impossible.

Here is a picture of the complete destitution of the times. "For a long time Israel was without the true God, without a priest to teach and without the law" (v. 3). Chronologically, the "long time" was a period of thirty years. It is because of the length of the spiritual drought that the very first sign of abundance is welcomed like a descending rain from heaven. When the flame of fire strikes dry wood, the effect is immediate and profound. But when religion is commonplace, there can be no revival. When everyone supposes that he knows everything that can be known and has what he needs, instruction is impossible. Consider the miracles of Christ— self-righteous men looked on in wonder with their eyes but refused to believe in their hearts that the source was divine.

Azariah appears as that great contrasting figure, so unlike everyone around him, and his speech is unlike all others' speech. Not only did Israel not have God, but the people had acquired innumerable gods of their own. They had no one to teach them the law of the one true God and help them understand it. Azariah brought the only message worth delivering, the only speech really worth listening to, and that is the speech that begins in eternity, sweeps down upon time, and leaves behind immortal lessons. He brings divine water to people who are thirsty, and who know the value of it, and after they have quenched their thirst, see how they respond. He goes to the people with broken hearts, contrite spirits, yearning for their souls, and they know it.

"When Asa heard these words and the prophecy of Azariah son of Oded the prophet, he took courage. He removed the detestable idols from the whole land . . . he repaired the altar of the LORD that was in front of the portico of the LORD's temple. . . . They took an oath to the LORD with loud acclamation, with shouting and with trumpets and horns. All Judah rejoiced about the oath because they had sworn it wholeheartedly. They sought God eagerly, and he was found by them. So the LORD gave them rest on every side" (vv. 8, 14-15).

It is a wonderful experience to be caught up in the full range of the genuine human and spiritual movement that was demonstrated here. Certainly, we recognize that there is an excitement that is false and inappropriate, where demonstrations of emotion are confused with true spirituality. But excitement of a genuine kind, balanced by reason and inspired by gratitude, sparkling with tears of the heart, is almost essential to our higher spiritual education. The people could not be content with their own voices. This self-impatience or self-discontentment has to do with the development of our best nature. We sometimes cannot explain what we are feeling; our voices are not enough. Trumpets and horns must be added. If we could, we would add thunder and lightning and all heaven's resources to express the love for God that burns with thanksgiving in our hearts. Such emotion will be disgusting to us if our soul is not in the same key. A heart sunk in worldliness cannot rise to such heights of worship.

On the other hand, it is a mistake to think that there can be no spiritual life, of the highest and purest and tenderest kind, apart from a loud voice with trumpets. True spirituality is not exhaustively defined by either one experience or another. Some people mistake what in reality is spiritual death and indifference and call it peace and restfulness of soul. Others pretend that you can live on nothing but constant excitement, but experience tells you that the foam and the froth never satisfy the hunger of your soul. Whatever touches the heart in man, whether it is quiet and meditative or loud and expressive, is the essential thing to his spiritual life. There is a middle lane in life, but that middle lane would become monotonous if we could not occasionally ascend and vary our progress, and return to the great average scheme and thought of life with renewed power and hope.

LIFE LESSON

· · · · · · · · · · · · · · · · ● ● ● · · · · · · · · · · · · · · · ·

Do not leave Pentecost out of your New Testament or your life! The Spirit of God desires to come into your life and transform it. Every soul needs to join Azariah and have its Pentecostal day. We need it to fall back upon sometimes when the devil comes against us with accusations about the validity of our relationship with God. There must be a time when we saw God—it may have been but for a moment, a flash, an unmeasurable period of time, but the sight is an everlasting memory and should be a steadfast and inexhaustible inspiration.

JOSEPH PARKER

BARTIMAEUS

The Nobody Who Wouldn't Stop Shouting

Then they came to Jericho. As Jesus and his disciples,
together with a large crowd, were leaving the city, a blind man,
Bartimaeus (that is, the Son of Timaeus), was sitting by the roadside
begging. When he heard that it was Jesus of Nazareth, he began to
shout, "Jesus, Son of David, have mercy on me!"

Many rebuked him and told him to be quiet,
but he shouted all the more, "Son of David, have mercy on me!"

Jesus stopped and said, "Call him."

So they called to the blind man,
"Cheer up! On your feet! He's calling you."

Throwing his cloak aside, he jumped to his feet and came to Jesus.

"What do you want me to do for you?" Jesus asked him.

The blind man said, "Rabbi, I want to see."

"Go," said Jesus, "your faith has healed you." Immediately he
received his sight and followed Jesus along the road.

MARK 10:46-52

. . . . ● ● ● ● ● . . . .

MARK'S ACCOUNT OF THE HEALING of Bartimaeus is evidently that of an eyewitness. It is full of little particulars that would come from someone who was there and witnessed the miracle. Remember that Jesus was now on His last journey to Jerusalem. That night He would sleep at Bethany; Calvary was but a week off. He had already paused to win Zacchaeus, who had climbed a tree to see Him, and now Jesus was resuming His march to His cross. An enthusiastic crowd was surging all around

Him, and for the first time He does not try to repress it. A shouting multitude is escorting Him out of the city. They have just passed the gates and are about to turn toward the mountain gorge through which the Jerusalem road runs.

As usual in the cities at that time, a long line of beggars is sitting outside the gate, well accustomed to lift their monotonous wail at the sound of passing footsteps. Bartimaeus is but one obscure nobody among a host of beggars hoping for a coin or a morsel of food from passersby. He asks, according to Luke (Luke 18:35-43), what is the cause for all the commotion, and is told, "Jesus of Nazareth is passing by" (v. 37). The name awakens strange hopes in him, which can only be accounted for by his knowledge of Christ's miracles done elsewhere. Long before this, Jesus' fame for healing the sick had spread through the whole land. It is a witness to His popularity among the masses that His miracles had filtered down to be the talk of beggars at city gates. And so, true to his position in life, Bartimaeus cries out, "Jesus . . . have mercy on me!"

Now, note two or three things about that cry. The first is the clear insight into Christ's place and dignity. The multitude said to him, "Jesus of Nazareth is passing by." That is all they cared for or knew. But Bartimaeus's cry is, "Jesus, Son of David, have mercy on me!" (v. 48). That cry distinctly recognized the Lord's Messianic character, His power and authority, and on that power and authority Bartimaeus built a confidence. He was sure that Jesus had both the power and the desire to heal him.

It is interesting to notice this same clear insight in other blind men in the evangelist's story. Blindness has its compensations. It leads to a certain steadfast brooding upon thoughts, free from disturbing influences. Seeing Jesus did not always produce faith in people; yet not seeing Him seems to have helped others. The lack of sight left the imagination to work undisturbed, and Jesus was all the more lofty to them because the conceptions of their minds were not limited by the vision of their eyes. This miracle gives insight into Christ's dignity, power, and will, to which the seeing multitudes swarming around Jesus were blind to.

Within Bartimaeus's desperate cry throbs a deep and urgent need. His loud plea shows that he realized the possibility that the amazing stories of healings that he had heard might be granted to him. He individualizes himself, *his* need, trusting in Christ's power and willingness to help *him*. And because he has heard of so many who have, in like manner, received His healing touch, Bartimaeus comes with the cry, "Have mercy on me!"

Bartimaeus's cry can be a mirror in which we may see ourselves, our needs, and the example of what our desire ought to be. The deep awareness of our spiritual powerlessness, need, emptiness, and blindness lies at the bottom of all true crying out to Jesus Christ for the help only He can give. If you have never gone to Him, knowing you're a sinful person, in peril, present and future, from your sin, and stained and marred because of it, then you never have gone to Him in any deep and adequate sense at all. Is the depth of your need as desperate as Bartimaeus so that from the core of your being you have to cry out, "Son of David, have mercy on me!"?

This poor beggar's cry expressed a true understanding of Jesus' unique character and power as the Son of David. Regal power was His both on earth and in heaven because of who He was, the Incarnate Word of God. Yet those around Bartimaeus tried to stifle his cry. It says, "Many rebuked him and told him to be quiet" (v. 48). The crowd sought to silence the persistent, strident voice of this Bible nobody whose annoying voice was piercing through their hosannas. They did not know that the poor cry of wretchedness was far sweeter to Him than their shallow hallelujahs. But Bartimaeus was not about to lose this once-in-a-lifetime opportunity. So he was persistently bold and shameless as he continued to cry out for mercy. The more they tried to silence him, the more he shouted.

Suddenly, Jesus stands still and commands for Bartimaeus to be brought to Him. Remember that He was on His road to His cross, and the teeming crowds all around Him had no idea of the tension of spirit He must have been feeling. Yet as absorbed as He must have been as His hour of death approached, Jesus did hear the blind beggar's cry, and He stopped His march in order to attend to it. Jesus Christ is not a dead Christ who is to only be remembered by us. He is a living Christ who, at this very moment, is all that He ever was, and is still doing all that He did when He walked on the earth.

That compassionate pause of the King is repeated now, and the attentive ear that was quick to discern the difference between the unreal shouts of the crowd, and the agony of sincerity in the cry of the beggar, is still open to hear our needs today. He does not need to pause in order to hear you and me. Nor can all the noise of our modern society that bombards our lives from all sides deafen His ears to our heart's cry. The writer of Hebrews tells us that His throne is open 24/7 for whatever need we have: "Therefore, since we have a great high priest who has gone through the heavens, Jesus the Son of God, let us hold firmly to the faith we profess. For we do not have a high priest who is unable to sympathize with our weaknesses, but we have one who has been tempted in every way, just as we are—yet was without sin. Let us then approach the throne of grace with confidence, so that we may receive mercy and find grace to help us in our time of need" (Hebrews 4:14-16).

The living Christ is as ready to help us immediately as He was outside the city gate of Jericho that day. And when they told Bartimaeus that Jesus was calling for him, what did he do? He sprang to his feet and threw away the rags that he had wrapped around him for warmth. Jesus waits, and when Bartimaeus approaches, He says, "What do you want me to do for you?" The exchange between them is brief, for Bartimaeus simply says, "I want to see."

And then the very thing that always delighted Jesus, and often was found where least expected, is seen in His response, " 'Go,' said Jesus, 'your *faith* has healed you.' Immediately he received his sight and followed Jesus along the road" (v. 52). Jesus saw the faith that Bartimaeus had and could not help but honor it. For the first time in his life, Bartimaeus opens his eyes and sees Jesus, the Son of David, who took time to stop and hear his cry for mercy. And Bartimaeus did what we must all do when Jesus touches our lives; "he received his sight and followed Jesus along the road" (v. 52).

LIFE LESSON

Whatever our need is today, Jesus hears our cry and is always ready to help us. Our part is to abandon whatever weighs us down and come in faith to Him. We must trust in Him in order that we may partake of the salvation He offers us by His power, His love, and His work on the cross. The condition for us is *faith*; the power comes from Him. Our faith is the hand that grasps His; it is His hand, not ours, that holds us up. If you will toss away your hindrances, your warm and comfortable rags of sin, and come and fall down before Him, knowing the depth of your need for mercy, He will save you and touch you with His healing grace right now!

ALEXANDER MACLAREN

BARUCH

The Nobody Whose Pen Worked Overtime

*In the fourth year of Jehoiakim son of Josiah king of Judah, this word
came to Jeremiah from the LORD: "Take a scroll and write on it all the
words I have spoken to you concerning Israel, Judah and all the other
nations from the time I began speaking to you in the reign of Josiah
till now. Perhaps when the people of Judah hear about every disaster
I plan to inflict on them, each of them will turn from his wicked way;
then I will forgive their wickedness and their sin."*

*So Jeremiah called Baruch son of Neriah, and while Jeremiah dictated
all the words the LORD had spoken to him, Baruch wrote them on the
scroll. Then Jeremiah told Baruch, "I am restricted; I cannot go to the
LORD's temple. So you go to the house of the LORD on a day of fasting
and read to the people from the scroll the words of the LORD that you
wrote as I dictated. Read them to all the people of Judah who come in
from their towns. Perhaps they will bring their petition before the
LORD, and each will turn from his wicked ways, for the anger and
wrath pronounced against this people by the LORD are great."*

*Baruch son of Neriah did everything Jeremiah the prophet told him
to do; at the LORD's temple he read the words of the LORD from the scroll.*

JEREMIAH 36:1-8

· · · · · · · · · · · · · · · · · ● ● ● ● · · · · · · · · · · · · · · · · ·

THE SCRIBES ARE OFTEN MENTIONED both in the Old
Testament and in the New. In the Gospels they almost
always appear in a bad light, as false and misleading teachers, and as opposers of the Lord. In the Old Testament they appear
in a more favorable light. In the New Testament, their duty was to
copy out the law of God contained in the Jewish Scriptures, so
sometimes they are referred to as "lawyers." But this was not all

they did. They were expounders and teachers of the law as well. Ezra the scribe taught the people after their return from seventy years of captivity in Babylon; and so did the scribes in the time of Jesus. But by then they had fallen into the great fault of neglecting the Word of God for tradition and teaching "for doctrines the commandments of men" (Matthew 15:9, KJV).

Baruch, the son of Neriah, was nobody famous in his day. He was simply a man who had chosen to be a scribe and strove to carry out that vocation as best he could. He lived in the time of Jeremiah, and all we know of him is linked with the history of that prophet. Jeremiah is one of the greatest characters found in the Bible and held a unique position. God had appointed him before birth to be His instrument: "Before I formed you in the womb I knew you, before you were born I set you apart; I appointed you as a prophet to the nations" (Jeremiah 1:5). Baruch, in comparison, bore but a humble part; yet the greater light should not be allowed to eclipse the lesser. Jeremiah furnishes us with a superb example of a life given over to total obedience to God in the face of years of persecution; yet Baruch in his faithful service to this great prophet also teaches us a lesson as well.

"So Jeremiah called Baruch son of Neriah . . ." (Jeremiah 36:4). This is the first we hear of Baruch. The historical circumstances surrounding Baruch and Jeremiah will help us understand the kind of man Baruch was. Jeremiah, the prophet, who had long been delivering God's messages and warnings, was commanded in the fourth year of King Jehoiakim (king of Judah, the southern kingdom) to write in a book all the words that had come to him by divine revelation from God, in order that the house of Judah might once more hear God's warnings because of their sins (vv. 1-3). The intent was that they would hear of God's impending judgments and would repent and find forgiveness. But Jeremiah was "confined in the courtyard of guard in the royal palace of Judah" (Jeremiah 32:2).

Most likely he had been imprisoned because of offending the king by his words of impending judgment that he prophesied.

All through the history of both the northern kingdom (Israel) and the southern kingdom (Judah), there were false prophets who would prophesy what the kings wanted to hear. But Jeremiah was not out to win the popularity contest with anyone but God Himself. Jeremiah had committed himself to only say what the Lord revealed to him no matter what personal sacrifice it would cost him. As we will see, throughout his whole life, he proclaimed God's Word to a rebellious nation that refused to hear the Word of the Lord.

Jeremiah called Baruch to become his scribe, and "while Jeremiah dictated all the words the LORD had spoken to him, Baruch wrote them on the scroll" (v. 4). Now because Jeremiah was locked up, he could not, therefore, go and read the book in public. Baruch's writing down word by word what Jeremiah spoke was a humble service, yet because the words that fell from the lips of the prophet were the living words of the Lord to him, even this humble service of recording them was an honorable and holy work. No service that is the direct service of God, however insignificant it may appear in the eyes of men, can be other than honorable, especially if it relates to His *Word*.

In today's standard of success, climbing the corporate ladder with all its benefits promises to be the epitome of "having made it." Some of the benefits people long for on the way to success are money, power, and prestige. And often, they will do whatever it takes to attain them. If that's the case, then Jeremiah didn't seem to measure up on any counts. In fact, if he were around today, he would be considered a dismal failure by all appearances. His entire prophetic career, which lasted for about forty years during the reigns of the last five kings of Judah, was not marked by what we would consider success, fame, money, or prestige. He suffered greatly for delivering the Lord's judgments against the land. He was rejected by everybody: kings, false prophets, friends, family, priests, and even his neighbors. And he definitely was not rich but poor by any monetary consideration. But the wealth he had could not be bought by all the money in the world. He enjoyed a treasure that has no price tag with it: God's *favor*. Jeremiah enjoyed that favor because he was utterly faithful in his obedience to deliver God's Word to the nation, despite the consequences he would have to suffer.

Everyone in the entire nation would have heard of Jeremiah. He was not one to be associated with if your social reputation mattered to you. Knowing that, probably very few people trained as scribes hurried to line up for the job opening to become Jeremiah's scribe. The job didn't pay well, and the benefits included suffering, rejection, the threat of losing your life, and the constant displeasure of everyone around you. Seen in that light, it is much to Baruch's honor that he chose to accept the position and stay by Jeremiah's side when others forsook him. There is something to admire about that kind of faith and loyalty. Or it may be that Jeremiah had a choice, and that Baruch was chosen for his faithfulness. In either case, his name has been recorded in Scripture that we may know him as faithful and true and learn from his example.

Whether he had any choice or not, Jeremiah had no doubt about calling Baruch to become his personal assistant and scribe. Evidently Baruch was already established in the good opinion of the prophet. This is no light testimony to Baruch's character. The well-founded esteem of an eminent servant of God is always a precious thing. To be chosen by a man of God as a helper, in however humble a way, is a high honor. Some direct, and some obey; some speak, and some write; some are "shut up" by various hindrances, while others can go out and preach. God has different work for different servants, and it is our honor to serve Him in whatever task He has set before us. And when we accept our particular task and do it well with all those others who follow Him, then we become part of a divine orchestra that together produces a great symphony that carries the melody of His grace to the whole world.

Baruch carefully wrote down all the words that Jeremiah spoke upon a scroll. But his task was not yet done. The most trying part was yet to come. It was easy to sit in private with the prophet and record what he said. Perhaps no one else knew of it. That was a work that might be done in secret and with little danger. But anonymity was not what the Lord had in store for Baruch. After finishing writing all the words of the Lord that Jeremiah spoke, the prophet told Baruch to take the scroll and read it in public, in the Lord's house, in the ears of all the people. And that was not going to be an easy task, for the prophecy he had to deliver was not one of blessing, but of imminent judgment for the wickedness in the land.

It is not clear from the history whether the scroll was read once or twice. If twice, then it was read first immediately after it was written, in the fourth year of Jehoiakim, at the great fast of the Jewish year, and again almost a year later, in the fifth year of Jehoiakim, on the occasion of a special fast, proclaimed by authority. Whether the scroll had been read before or not, it was certainly read in the fifth year of Jehoiakim, in the ninth month (Jeremiah 36:9).

It is believed that it was between the writing of the scroll and this reading of it that Nebuchadnezzar, king of Babylon, came and conquered Jerusalem as Jeremiah had prophesied (Jeremiah 21:10). It was soon after this great humiliation that a great national fast was proclaimed, and it was then that the scroll was read. This was no common occasion. The fast that was proclaimed was not only for the people of Jerusalem, but also for all those who came from the cities of Judah (Jeremiah 36:9). People flocked to Jerusalem from every part of the country. At this time Baruch was to read the scroll. How would the people respond? A fast day does not always bring humility and penitence. It may well be that in that great gathering there was much wounded pride and fierce rebellion

of spirit. Would the people patiently hear of their faults after seeing what the Babylonians had done to them? Would they listen
humbly to God's denunciations of their sins that had brought judgment? Would Baruch, the messenger, be safe? If such thoughts
occurred to Baruch, he did not yield to them. The narrative is very
simple: "From the room of Gemariah son of Shaphan the secretary,
which was in the upper courtyard at the entrance of the New Gate
of the temple, Baruch read to all the people at the LORD's temple the
words of Jeremiah from the scroll" (v. 10).

Baruch had probably never before addressed so great a multitude, or filled so prominent a place; yet he did not shrink from the
task. Baruch read the solemn words of the Lord just as they were
written. He did not soften those strong indictments or leave out
one word of what God had said. Among the hearers was a young
man Mechaiah, son to that Gemariah in whose chamber the roll
was read. His father and the other princes were not present, so he
went and told them what Baruch had just read. They called for
Baruch to read the prophecy to them, too. When they heard all the
words, they were afraid. If it was a trial of Baruch's courage and
faithfulness to stand and read the scroll to the people, it was even
more difficult to read it to this council of princes. This narrative
gives us a glimpse of his courage and the absolute confidence in
the validity of the message he had written down. Upon hearing the
troubling words, their advice was that Jeremiah and Baruch should
hide themselves from the persecution that would surely come. The
text says that the Lord himself "hid them" (v. 26, KJV).

When the king heard the words written in the scroll, he became
enraged and burnt the scroll (Jeremiah 36:20-23). The very next
thing we read of is another scroll and another message. Baruch was
instructed to write another scroll similar to the one that had been
burnt, but this new scroll now contained a severe judgment on the
king for having burnt the Word of the Lord. So far we have learned

nothing beyond the outward conduct of Baruch. We have seen him faithfully taking part with Jeremiah and showing boldness and steadfastness in doing what he was given to do. He surely had his dark moments, because he believed that all that God said would come true. So he was deeply afflicted at what was coming on his people. And now he was in danger of his life as well and had to hide from the wrath of the king.

Even when Baruch vented his fear about being killed, God gave a message to Jeremiah to tell Baruch that He would protect him (Jeremiah 45:1-5). The eye of God was upon the humble scribe as well as upon the great prophet. He who cared for Baruch cares for every faithful servant of His in distress. None are overlooked, and not a thought or a feeling is disregarded. God sent that special word to Baruch to assure him that He was with him as well as Jeremiah, and that his life would be spared.

About seventeen years pass, and then we hear of Baruch once more in the sacred history. Even after all those years, he has remained faithfully beside Jeremiah. And now he has become more than a scribe to Jeremiah. He has taken on the role of advisor (Jeremiah 43), giving the prophet counsel that the people should stay in the land and submit to the Babylonians rather than flee to Egypt.

God took a faithful servant who for years had humbly filled his office as scribe in the shadows of a great prophet and turned him into a trusted adviser. Baruch, who otherwise would have been anonymous, in the end won for himself a respected influence with others beyond what his station in life would have normally given him.

LIFE LESSON

．．．．．．．．．．．．．．．．．．．●●●●●．．．．．．．．．．．．．．．．．．

Boldly proclaiming the Word of God will have a price tag in our generation just as it did in the days of Jeremiah and Baruch. *Sin* and *repentance* are not popular words these days. But God's conditions to restore fellowship with Him haven't changed in 2,500 years. Confession, forsaking sin, and turning back in repentance to God through faith in Jesus Christ is the only way to restore that broken relationship. And we are called to be faithful like Jeremiah and Baruch and spread that message of reconciliation to others as Paul says: "All this is from God, who reconciled us to himself through Christ and gave us the ministry of reconciliation" (2 Corinthians 5:18). And no matter what dangers, temptations, or tribulations we face, He has promised to never leave us, nor forsake us, and that He will save us to the uttermost (Hebrews 13:5; 7:25).

FRANCIS BOURDILLON

BARZILLAI

The Nobody Who Was Always There for His Friends

When David came to Mahanaim, Shobi son of Nahash from Rabbah of the Ammonites, and Makir son of Ammiel from Lo Debar, and Barzillai the Gileadite from Rogelim brought bedding and bowls and articles of pottery. They also brought wheat and barley, flour and roasted grain, beans and lentils, honey and curds, sheep, and cheese from cows' milk for David and his people to eat. For they said, "The people have become hungry and tired and thirsty in the desert."

2 SAMUEL 17:27-29

. . . . ● ● ● ● ● . . . .

BARZILLAI, TO PUT IT ALL INTO ONE WORD, was an aged, venerable, wealthy, hospitable Highland chief. By this time, he was eighty years old, and he was full of truth, courage, goodness, and generosity. From within the walls of his lofty stronghold in far-off Gilead, Barzillai had watched the ways of God with His people Israel in the south country all through the days of Eli, Samuel, Saul, David, Joab, Jonathan, Mephibosheth, and Absalom, and his humble heart and his hospitable house had always been open to the oppressed and persecuted and poor. And thus it was that when David fled from Jerusalem to escape from his son Absalom, and when David made his final stand at Mahanaim, Barzillai was quick in coming to David's assistance, replenishing the king's badly depleted camp. As he was coming to the twilight of life, you would expect someone his age to gracefully slip from history's pages into anonymity. But not so with Barzillai. Age might have been weakening his body, but it would never sap the strength of his loyalty to help David in whatever way he could.

Then came David's victory over Absalom and his return to

Jerusalem. At the Jordan River he is met by Barzillai, and David offers to have Barzillai come and stay with him in Jerusalem. In remembrance of Barzillai's gracious provision at a time of need, David offers to provide for his friend for the rest of his life. Barzillai's grateful response is that he is far too old to come and that his only wish is to return home and eventually be put to rest with his forefathers (2 Samuel 19:34-37). This is a beautiful old man and a beautiful incident during what was a far from beautiful time in David's life.

Barzillai was a true Highlander in his splendid loyalty to David in his distress. Many men who sat at David's royal table held back until David had overthrown the conspiracy against him. There were many reasons why a deliberating man should stand aloof for a time from a man such as David who had done so much to bring on his own fall. But the old hero from Gilead took his ancient tower, his great estate, his own future, and the future of his family all in his hand that day and remained faithful to David. Barzillai had steered all his eighty years by the fixed stars of truth, righteousness, duty, and loyalty, and he would steer by the same stars to the end. David, on the throne or off the throne, in Jerusalem or in Mahanaim, is our king, said Barzillai to his household.

And, every day, we all have Barzillai's duty and opportunity too, if only we have Barzillai's mind and heart. There is not a day that passes but our boldness, courage, loyalty, and fidelity are put to the test, whether it is through the support of a good cause, a needy and deserving person, or old and distressed friends. And what do we do? Do we silently, or with a half-uttered consent, give in to fault-finding and harmful words about our friends? Let us be honorable the next time. Let us be Barzillai the next time and take our stand with them.

Barzillai also shows his truly Highland courtesy in anticipating David's needs and being there to meet them as best he can. In hospitality e did for David as David would have done for him. You cannot tie up the hands of a hospitable heart like Barzillai's. Generosity and magnanimity are in the mind and in the heart, and it is the mind and the heart that are accepted and acknowledged of God. And then with what sweetness of manner and speech he excused himself out of all the royal rewards and honors that David had designed for him. Barzillai carries with himself a New Testament humility in its depths and beauty that go down into the grace of God.

LIFE LESSON

A t eighty years of age, wise and good Barzillai is surely a beautiful lesson to us all. He shows us how to apply wisdom to our hearts as we number our days. He shows us how, with all willingness and sweetness, to leave cities and feasts and honors and promotions and to apply our whole remaining strength and time to end our days as our days should be ended. Barzillai, having showed us how to live, shows us how to die. Barzillai dies the same devout and noble and magnanimous man he has all his days lived.

JOSEPH PARKER

BENAIAH

The Nobody Who Would Make a Good Recon Marine

Benaiah son of Jehoiada was a valiant fighter from Kabzeel, who
performed great exploits. He struck down two of Moab's best men. He
also went down into a pit on a snowy day and killed a lion. And he
struck down an Egyptian who was seven and a half feet tall.
Although the Egyptian had a spear like a weaver's rod in his hand,
Benaiah went against him with a club. He snatched the spear from
the Egyptian's hand and killed him with his own spear. Such were the
exploits of Benaiah son of Jehoiada; he too was as famous as the
three mighty men. He was held in greater honor than any of the
Thirty, but he was not included among the Three. And David put him
in charge of his bodyguard.

1 CHRONICLES 11:22-25

· · · · · · · · · · · · · · · · · ● ● ● ● ● · · · · · · · · · · · · · · · · ·

BENAIAH WAS THE SON OF JEHOIADA and became
renowned as a valiant fighter for David. He was the ancient
equivalent of today's Recon Marines or Army Rangers—not
someone you even think about messing around with! If you saw
him coming in your direction, the wisest move would be to get out
of his way. Benaiah probably started out just like the other common lads in his tribe, but something inside him stirred him to
greater ideals. And because of his determination to always
improve, he went from one of the boys to one of the valiant warriors. A real nobody who rose from the ranks of mediocrity to
become the man in charge of David's bodyguard.

Other translations of verse 22 state that Benaiah was "the son
of a valiant man of Kabzeel," indicating that the valiant son followed a valiant father. If the virtues of the fathers were always

repeated in the sons, what wonderful progress the ages of civilization would have seen. But the fact remains that whatever a father is able to pass along to his children, he is unable to impart to them the character and integrity that he himself has acquired. Every child must learn the alphabet of life for himself. Some similarities of personality may be traceable to heredity, but the full development of that personality must be exercised by its owner on quite independent grounds. We cannot live long on the reputation of our father.

The reality is that several generations may pass in decline, but then a man arises who surprises the ages by remarkable giftings and transcendent valor of every kind. Providence seems to rebuke everything of personal vanity in this regard, raising up and casting down by an uncontrollable law, and thus preserving a wonderful equality among men, even in the midst of apparent inequalities that would seem to separate people by impassable distances. Every person needs to realize that no matter what their earthly parentage has been, he or she has a greater Father in heaven to whom he or she is responsible.

So what did Benaiah do to create for himself a place in history? Three major deeds are represented in the biblical text as having been accomplished by this valiant man: (1) He struck down two renowned warriors of Moab; (2) he went down into a snowy pit and killed a lion; (3) and he brought down a seven-and-half-foot-tall Egyptian warrior. At the time that he accomplished these feats, the stories probably spread through the nation like fire and were built up to the point of his being a living legend. The fact that he was honored to become the head of David's bodyguard indicates that his exploits were not limited to these three outstanding feats of strength and valor.

In a spiritual sense, we, too, are called upon to join Benaiah and slay, destroy, and overthrow. Are you anxious to slay a lion? "Be self-controlled and alert. Your enemy the devil prowls around like a roaring lion looking for someone to devour" (1 Peter 5:8). There is a lion that each of us must fight, and there is no escaping him. Are we inclined to go out and search for the nest of the serpent and destroy the horrible creature? Satan is described as "the serpent," and from the beginning "was more crafty than any of the wild animals the LORD God had made" (Genesis 3:1). The Son of Man came to crush the head of the serpent, and we are called upon to take part in the great destruction (Genesis 3:15).

The battle has only changed its ground, its scope, and its purpose since the valiant days of Benaiah. Life is still a tremendous fight, though we may never fight renowned warriors of Moab or seven-footers from Egypt. The weapons of our warfare are spiritual, but they are not, therefore, the less weapons of war, and our warfare is not the less warfare. "Therefore put on the full armor of God, so that when the day of evil comes, you may be able to stand your ground, and after you have done everything, to stand" (Ephesians 6:13). Enemies are far more mischievous and deadly when they are invisible, striking without warning and with schemes tested over dark centuries. This is the enemy we face.

Lest we take our enemy lightly, let us consider his deeds as a roaring lion. He deceived Adam and Eve, and thus brought sin and death upon them and the rest of humankind (Genesis 3). He moved David to number the people (1 Chronicles 21:1), bringing on divine judgment. He accused Joshua the high priest before the angel of the Lord (Zechariah 3:1). He tempted Jesus Christ (Matthew 4); entered into Judas Iscariot, to persuade him to betray his master (Luke 22:3); instigated Ananias and Sapphira to lie to the Holy Spirit (Acts 5:3); hindered Paul and Barnabas on their way to the Thessalonians (1 Thessalonians 2:18). He is the spirit that now works in those who are disobedient (Ephesians 2:2); he is the deceiver of the world (Revelation 12:9); and he has the power to work all kinds of counterfeit miracles, signs, and wonders (2 Thessalonians 2:9).

The means that the devil uses are variously called schemes, flaming arrows, traps, and all deceivableness of unrighteousness.

He darkens the understanding of men to keep them in ignorance. He perverts their judgments that he may lead them into error. He instills evil thoughts and thereby awakens impure desires. He excites them to pride, anger, and revenge; to discontentment, gloom, and rebellion. He labors to prop up false systems of religion and to corrupt and overturn the true one. He came into direct conflict with the Savior in the temptations in the desert, hoping to draw Him from His allegiance to God and win worship for himself. When that ploy failed, he instigated the Jews to put Jesus to death, thinking to defeat His designs and plans. Here, too, satan failed and was made to subserve the very redemptive ends that he desperately wanted to prevent.

Christians are called upon to fight against self-indulgence, to crucify the flesh with its desires, to keep themselves in check, "so that after I have preached to others, I myself will not be disqualified for the prize" (1 Corinthians 9:27). They are not to be conformed to the world, but to be transformed, by the renewing of their minds, by the creation of a new conscience, a new purpose, and a new will in life (Romans 12:2). They are to see the temporariness of all things earthly; they are to use those things but not abuse them. Christians are called to fight a battle every day against the insidious attacks of worldly ambition. They are to go out and seek those who are lost. They are to let the mind of Christ be in them, that being joined to Christ in His humiliation they may be raised with Him in His glory and honor (Philippians 2:5-11).

Benaiah was beautifully described as a "valiant fighter." This is what the Church needs now, both in the pulpit and in the pew. This is no time for indifference, fearfulness, self-consideration, or cowardliness. The devil plans his evil schemes at the corners of the street, being the first up in the morning and last out at night, studying the tastes of people and accommodating himself to them. There is no person, however high or low, whose strengths and weaknesses he does not study with a view to corruption and overthrow. The

Church requires valiant fighters and exemplary champions who defeat the enemy at every point of attack.

All men are not valiant in the same direction, any more than they are valiant in the same degree. One man is valiant in bringing the gospel into the public forum: give him a sword and let him fight his battle in his own way. Another man is valiant in prayer: let him also have his sword and fight his secret battle in the solitude of prayer. Another is brilliant in leading and inspiring others in the great battle for righteousness and purity and love. It is a pitiable day for the Church when she forgets that though the regiments are many the army is one. Is it a time to be fighting over uniforms, badges, and awards of distinction, when the enemy is at the gate, his mouth filled with boasting, and his eyes blazing with malignant passion? Let us forget all petty theological separations, all merely regimental distinctions and honors, and gather together into one great force to strike a united blow at a common enemy.

God does not evaluate His people by the things that are seen. He knows who are heroic in heart, and He writes down the inward proofs of heroism as if they were accomplished facts. He knows who would give much if he had much to give, and He sets down in His book a great sum as if it had actually been contributed. God knows every spiritual battle that is proceeding in the heart, in the family, in the Church, and in the world. The day will come when many shall be found who have been giants and heroes, mighty and valiant men and women, who have been regarded in this life as timid, silent, and almost useless nobodies. Look into your heart and see what you discover. Every person knows in their own heart what they are, what they would be, and what they would do if they could. We need not wait for the least illumination to throw light upon our own character, because at this moment we may see it just as it is, if we really want to do so, and will study ourselves at the cross of Christ.

LIFE LESSON

· · · · · · · · · · · · · · · · ● · ● ● · ● · · · · · · · · · · · · · · · ·

We do not need to lament that the valiant days of Benaiah's military exploits are behind us. These are still days of storm and tempest, days of heroism and chivalry. Truly there is an unprecedented spiritual battle going on all around us. If you have determined to take your stand with Jesus Christ, you have found that you must have a sword in your right hand, and that even while you sleep, you must have your armor so near that at a moment's notice you can jump back into the battle. The roaring lion who was not afraid to bring his temptation to one as mighty as the Lord Jesus will certainly bring his battle to you. "Put on the full armor of God so that you can take your stand against the devil's schemes" (Ephesians 6:11).

JOSEPH PARKER

CLEOPAS *and* HIS COMPANION

The Nobodies Who Had the Shock of Their Life

Now that same day two of them were going to a village called Emmaus, about seven miles from Jerusalem. They were talking with each other about everything that had happened. As they talked and discussed these things with each other, Jesus himself came up and walked along with them; but they were kept from recognizing him.

He asked them, "What are you discussing together as you walk along?"

They stood still, their faces downcast. One of them, named Cleopas, asked him, "Are you only a visitor to Jerusalem and do not know the things that have happened there in these days?"

LUKE 24:13-18

. . . . ● ● ● ● ● . . . .

CLEOPAS AND HIS COMPANION were two ordinary men from Emmaus who had gone up to Jerusalem the week before to keep the Passover, as was their tradition. They were disciples of our Lord. Their names were not among the twelve apostles, but it is very likely they were well known among the seventy-two that had been sent out to preach the good news of the gospel (Luke 10:1). They had gone up to the feast in the hope that Jesus would be there, and that they would see and hear Him as they had in the past. But now it seemed to them like a year, like a lifetime, like another world, since last week when they had walked and talked together, so full of hope and expectation, all the way up from Emmaus to Jerusalem.

Jesus had come up to the Passover just as they had expected He would. During that last week, they had both seen Him and had heard Him speak. They had followed Him about in the streets of Jerusalem as He preached His last sermons. Neither of them had been invited to the upper room, but they had done the next best thing. They had celebrated the Passover, and then learned late that night that Jesus had been betrayed by one His disciples and was at that very moment in the hands of His enemies and on trial.

With their Passover staffs in their hands, Cleopas and his companion walked the streets of Jerusalem all that night and till after the crucifixion was finished. By the third day an indescribable sickness of heart had overwhelmed Cleopas, and at last he said to his companion, "It is time to go. Let us shake the dust off our feet against this accursed city and leave."

Certain women of their company had rushed into the city that morning all excited, saying that they had seen a vision of angels who told them that their crucified Master had risen from the dead and left His grave. But to Cleopas's heavy heart their words were nothing but idle tales. "No, no!" Cleopas said to his companion. "It's time for us to return home. Believe me, we have seen the last of the redemption of Israel in our day."

Why was Cleopas in such a hurry to get home? Couldn't he have gone out to see the empty grave himself? Surely he could have waited in Jerusalem until the end of "the third day" that his Master so often foretold about Himself? But Cleopas's despair and despondency were so great that he only wanted to return to the familiarity and security of his home. As they made their way back to Emmaus, they walked and talked together about everything that had happened during that Passover. And the farther they got from Jerusalem, the more their hearts were burdened beneath an unbearable yoke of sorrow. When Jesus was crucified on Golgotha, all their hopes died that day as well.

Suddenly a stranger overtook them as they reasoned and debated together in their sadness.

"Peace be with you both!" said the stranger with a pleasant voice as he joined himself to their company.

But Cleopas was scarcely even civil. He hardly returned the stranger's greeting, so overwhelmed was he with his sadness and grief. And for a while they all walked on in silence. Finally the sympathizing stranger broke the sad silence.

"Why do you seem so sad, my friends?"

"Are you such a stranger in Jerusalem," answered Cleopas, "that you do not know all that has happened there in these days? Where were you all last week? Where were you on the eve of Sabbath? You couldn't have been in Jerusalem, for the whole city was out at Calvary that morning. And if you had been there, you would not wonder at our sadness."

The stranger did not say whether he had been out at Calvary last Friday morning or not.

"What things?" he asked, bowing, as it were, to Cleopas's reproof and reproach at such unaccountable ignorance at such a time.

And then we have Cleopas's reply in his own words, recorded by Luke. " 'About Jesus of Nazareth,' they replied. 'He was a prophet, powerful in word and deed before God and all the people. The chief priests and our rulers handed him over to be sentenced to death, and they crucified him; but we had hoped that he was the one who was going to redeem Israel. And what is more, it is the third day since all this took place. In addition, some of our women amazed us. They went to the tomb early this morning but didn't find his body. They came and told us that they had seen a vision of angels, who said he was alive. Then some of our companions went to the tomb and found it just as the women had said, but him they did not see' " (Luke 24:19-24).

To their amazement, the stranger then demonstrated a keen knowledge of the very Scriptures they had been speaking about. Immediately, He began showing them from Moses and the writings of the Prophets how the Christ must suffer and enter into His glory through the agony of the cross. What an eye-opening hour that must have been to Cleopas and his companion! They soon forgot about themselves and were carried captive with this stranger's remarkable knowledge, with His supreme authority, and with His burning words. And it's no wonder their hearts stirred with excitement. Many highly educated and earnest and eloquent men have expounded on Moses and David and Isaiah since that Emmaus afternoon. But human ears and human hearts have never heard such another exposition of Holy Scripture as Cleopas and his friend heard from that stranger's lips.

This stranger seemed to have all the Scriptures within Himself. Somehow He knew Moses, and David, and Isaiah, and Jeremiah absolutely by heart. And the manner in which He spoke to them called to their remembrance all that they had ever heard or read in Moses, and the Prophets, and the Psalms: the seed of the woman; the brazen serpent; the paschal lamb; He was wounded for our transgressions, He was bruised for our iniquities. . . .

Never did seven miles from Jerusalem to Emmaus seem so short that day. "Come and eat with us," said the entranced Cleopas to this mysterious stranger who had so overmastered him and set his heart ablaze. "Stay with us, for it is nearly evening." And when they had sat down to supper, Cleopas naturally asked the stranger, as you would have done, to say grace. Whatever the grace was that He said, you may be sure He did not say it as we say our graces. He did not mumble it over so that nobody could hear it. He did not say it as if He was ashamed of it. He blessed the bread and broke it and gave it to them. And suddenly their eyes were opened and they recognized the very Bread of Life who had walked with them, opened the Scriptures to them, and blessed them. And then He was gone!

If you see yourself wandering around in life in disappointment like these nobodies from Emmaus, I beg you to open your heart as they did to the Lord's burning words about Himself. Wherever you find yourself on the road of life, earnestly seek out someone who can open the Word of God to your heart. Do whatever it takes to put yourself where you can hear what Jesus wants to say to you. Jesus said, "The Spirit gives life; the flesh counts for nothing. The words I have spoken to you are spirit and they are life" (John 6:63). If by chance you enter a church on a Sunday with your heart sad, with your hopes crushed, with your expectations a complete shipwreck, like Cleopas and his desponding companion, and the preacher opens God's Word to you, setting forth the way of redemption, that your heart is set aflame all day, then stay there and listen carefully. "That is my servant for you," says your God to you. "I have made his mouth like a sharp sword for you." And that person you have just heard may be as great a stranger to you as our Lord was to Cleopas on that highway that afternoon. Do not leave their presence, but open your heart and let them break the Word of Life to your broken heart.

LIFE LESSON

· · · · · · · · · · · · · · ● ● ● · · · · · · · · · · · · ·

When life seems to deal a cruel blow and dashes your dreams to pieces, God has a unique way of bringing a message of hope and resurrection. But do not let yourself get bogged down by all of life's concerns or the very disappointment or failure that has placed you in despair. For sometimes from the least expected person at the most unexpected time God will speak and cause your heart to burn as Cleopas's and his friend's did when Jesus opened their understanding to the Scriptures. Remember that the Word of God is alive and powerful and will always bring life to your soul.

ALEXANDER WHYTE

THE DAUGHTER
of PHARAOH

The Nobody Who Couldn't Resist a Baby Boy

Then Pharaoh's daughter went down to the Nile to bathe, and her attendants were walking along the river bank. She saw the basket among the reeds and sent her slave girl to get it. She opened it and saw the baby. He was crying, and she felt sorry for him. "This is one of the Hebrew babies," she said.

Then his sister asked Pharaoh's daughter, "Shall I go and get one of the Hebrew women to nurse the baby for you?"

"Yes, go," she answered. And the girl went and got the baby's mother. Pharaoh's daughter said to her, "Take this baby and nurse him for me, and I will pay you." So the woman took the baby and nursed him. When the child grew older, she took him to Pharaoh's daughter and he became her son. She named him Moses, saying, "I drew him out of the water."

EXODUS 2:5-10

I T IS INTERESTING that the biblical narrative should shine its spotlight on an unnamed Egyptian princess to show us woman in her most divine capacity, acting as the servant of God to pity the helpless, save the perishing, and nourish an abandoned baby. That this most exquisite portrait of woman at her very best should be an Egyptian rather than an Israelite shows how impartial the sacred history is. The revelation of her sensitive character is so unerring and so charming, the incidents are told so simply, and the eternal significance of her doings is so unpretentiously indicated that she has much to teach us.

While the centuries-long debate continues as to which Pharaoh was her father, history tells us that women were far more liberated and independent in Egypt than in Eastern countries or even in the Greece of historical times. The preeminence of Egypt in antiquity is probably due at least in part to the establishment of women's rights in social and political life. It does not take a great intelligence to see that any nation, state, or society that degrades women can never flourish, whether it was four millenniums ago or today.

We cannot, however, assume she had any distinguished position at her father's court. If, for instance, her father was Rameses II as some theorize, he had one hundred eleven sons and fifty-one daughters. In a royal family so large, it is easily conceivable that she had hardly an acquaintance with her father. On the other hand, the fact that she went against his order of Hebrew infanticide need not lead us to suppose that there was any element of personal rebellion against him.

Concern over the swelling numbers of Hebrew slaves had caused Pharaoh's order to thin out the population. Accordingly, the male children are all committed to the Nile. The situation is all too imaginable. The sacred Nile swallows up the seed of Abraham, Isaac, and Jacob, devastating what remains of the spirit of the slaves. Every mother is hoping that her son may be the one who will deliver Israel; and one by one these hopes are quenched in despair as the man-child is snatched away and flung into the river.

Moses' mother, Jochebed, had hidden her baby boy for three months, but she knew this could not last. She then conceives of a plan whereby she might save her child, though it was possible she would never see him again. In a sublime motherly act, utterly unselfish, she was ready to give up all, even her own beloved child, if only he may live. If she could just get him in front of the right woman, she believed it would be impossible for the baby to be seen and not loved.

And yes, the infinite love of God was brooding over that helpless child, and with a design that no human being could conceive, He brings Pharaoh's daughter to the water's edge one day with a heart filled with compassion. The cry of the little child in the papyrus basket pierces her heart, and she is won over instantly. A tale of heroism is revealed here as she recognizes that this is a Hebrew child doomed to destruction by the irresistible will of her father, the Pharaoh. Such a stand could have easily cost her her life.

Here is a woman brought up in the worship of Ammon, nourished on the strange fantasies of Egyptian mythology, perhaps half believing that her father is divine. And yet her heart is so tender that it melts with compassion to save an innocent child, and so strong that it unhesitatingly resolves to face all risks in order to satisfy her compassion. And to the tenderness and courage of the heathen princess Moses owes his life; Moses, the great inspired lawgiver and prophet, the chosen mouthpiece of Yahweh, and the liberator of His people from the bondage of Egypt.

Certainly it is clear to Pharaoh's daughter who the sister and mother of Moses are. Yet she is willing to cast aside the prevailing prejudice and bring into her own royal household a slave, the offspring of a despised and even hated race. Imagine the walls of social distinction and superiority that she had to overcome within herself. It lights up this unnamed princess with the glory of an elevated character, bordering on the quality of sanctity. It reflects a deed of compassion that occurs only in characters of the finest mold.

And one other remark remains to be made. It was Pharaoh's daughter who gave the baby boy the name by which he has become one of the most famous men in history. There is evidence to show that Moses is a purely Egyptian and not a Hebrew name. It was the privilege of this noble woman to stamp history with a great name.

But it was also her merit, in part at least, to mold the man who has made the name itself great. Through her actions, Moses was brought up in the noblest schools and trained in the highest wisdom that the ancient world had then attained. She had much to do with the shaping of this man into the world leader and deliverer he ultimately became. Too bad we don't know her name. She truly deserves to be honored.

LIFE LESSON

· · · · · · · · · · · · · · · ● ● ● · · · · · · · · · · · · · ·

We only catch the silhouette of this Egyptian princess in a sidelight of history, but it is stamped upon the mind as one of the sweetest figures we know. Tenderness and courage fill the heart of a compassionate soul and lead to actions that transcend social distinctions and even legal mandates. When we reach out to the needy, in whatever loving capacity we may serve them, who can say what the results may be? Today's helpless child may become tomorrow's world shaper. Never underestimate the power of doing good.

Robert Horton

DEBORAH
the DELIVERER

The Nobody Who Loved to Sing

After Ehud died, the Israelites once again did evil in the eyes of the
LORD. So the LORD sold them into the hands of Jabin, a king of
Canaan, who reigned in Hazor. The commander of his army was
Sisera, who lived in Harosheth Haggoyim. Because he had nine hun-
dred iron chariots and had cruelly oppressed the Israelites for twenty
years, they cried to the LORD for help.

Deborah, a prophetess, the wife of Lappidoth, was leading Israel at
that time. She held court under the Palm of Deborah between Ramah
and Bethel in the hill country of Ephraim, and the Israelites came to
her to have their disputes decided. She sent for Barak son of Abinoam
from Kedesh in Naphtali and said to him, "The LORD, the God of
Israel commands you: 'Go, take with you ten thousand men of
Naphtali and Zebulun and lead the way to Mount Tabor. I will lure
Sisera, the commander of Jabin's army, with his chariots and his
troops to the Kishon River and give him into your hands.' "

JUDGES 4:1-7

· · · · · · · · · · · · · · · · · · ● ● ● · · · · · · · · · · · · · · · · · ·

THE HISTORY DURING THE INTERVAL between the
death of Joshua and the rise of Samuel reminds us, by a
rude shock, that even in the heart of God's chosen people,
even in the next generation after Joshua, there were imperfections
that required God's constant discipline. "In those days Israel had
no king; everyone did as he saw fit" is the keynote of the times
(Judges 17:6). It expresses the independence, the irresponsibility,
the anarchy, the disorder of the period. These troubled times often

produced judges, warrior heroes who rose up out of anonymity and would deliver the people from their oppressors.

The years of "rest" that the land of Israel enjoyed under Ehud's rule came to an end with his death, and the Israelites fell back into doing evil. The occasional spiritual fidelity of Israel had been triggered by Ehud's moral sway, but in his absence the undercurrent of distrust and idolatry resumed its influence throughout the land. But the presence of Sisera with nine hundred Canaanite chariots of iron intimidated the sinning Israelites, and for twenty long years he oppressed them cruelly. They forgot that God is able to break the chariots in pieces and to turn all their massive strength into a disadvantage and a difficulty, as when the Egyptians were mired down in the Red Sea and waves. The spirit of patriotism was dead in the land, and there was little to distinguish God's people from the people that surrounded them. Hearts that were once proud and free now shook with fear and lived in constant terror of the next military raid.

It was at this time that Deborah judged or ruled over Israel— not only the families near where she lived, but from far and near many came to seek the guidance and counsel of this woman. The reports of her wisdom and her zeal and devotion to Israel's God had traveled north and south and east and west; she judged Israel. A prophetic woman, a seer somewhat like what Samuel was in later times, not content to give direction to the people for a fee, she carried in her heart a passionate faith in Jehovah and His helping hand to deliver. The distress of the people and their dishonoring of God went straight to her heart. Her wrath was fierce against all who slipped aside from the worship of Jehovah, and all this spiritual passion mingled with her patriotic rage at the misery of her people to drive her into insurrection against the king of Canaan and his chariots of iron. She is the magnificent impersonation of the free spirit of the Jewish people and of Jewish life.

It was a great day for Israel when Deborah left the shadow of the palm tree and went northward to summon Barak to the defense of his people. It shows the commanding position to which Deborah had attained that Barak immediately responded to her word. And it is a further tribute to the remarkable personal influence of this woman that, when the matter was explained to Barak, he refused to join the military campaign unless they had the presence and the counsel of Deborah with them. Clearly, of all the souls in Israel this woman was the most dauntless, the most resolved and noble.

If you read the rest of the story of Deborah and Barak, you discover that Sisera, his nine hundred chariots, and vast numbers of Canaanites gathered in the plain of Esdraelon. Against them came the ten thousand poorly armed men of Israel at the command of Deborah and Barak. The battle at the waters of Megiddo was joined on level ground, and the Canaanites were thoroughly routed. We learn from Josephus, the Jewish historian, and indirectly from the Song of Deborah in Judges 5, that a tremendous storm of sleet and hail burst over the plain, driving full in the faces the advancing Canaanites and throwing them into confusion. The river Kishon rose to a torrent and the chariots became a liability, then the Canaanites turned to flee.

One of those who fled was Sisera, and he perished at the hands of another Bible nobody, Jael, just as Deborah had originally told Barak (Judges 4:9). No sooner was the deed done than Barak came by, hot in pursuit, and saw with joy that his foe lay dead. The same day Deborah met him, and the prophetess changed into the poet. She sang of the uprising, the battle, and the death of the enemy; and she uttered words of scorn and mockery rarely equaled in the literature of war. The passions roused by the battle were still warm in her song—the sense of a common danger, the enthusiasm of united action, the exultation of Jehovah's triumphant aid are felt with a vividness that only a participant could have given. The Song of Deborah was preeminently a battle song of triumph.

LIFE LESSON

· · · · · · · · · · · · · · · · ● ● ● · · · · · · · · · · · · · · ·

We see in the life of Deborah an inspired woman, one whose voice and manner are charged with the invisible presence of God. The ring in the great Song is authentic and overwhelming. The words roll with the majesty of natural forces and thunder with the voice of God. True love to God means a hearty hatred of all that opposes Him. If we would have Him as our God, if we would be free, we must put aside every fear and hindrance and sin that clings so closely to our sides. We must face every battle of soul and spirit with the same undaunting courage that Deborah faced the army of Sisera.

JAMES HASTINGS

DORCAS

The Nobody Who Could Sew Like Lightning

*In Joppa there was a disciple named Tabitha (which,
when translated, is Dorcas), who was always doing good
and helping the poor. About that time she became sick and died,
and her body was washed and placed in an upstairs room. Lydda was
near Joppa; so when the disciples heard that Peter was in Lydda, they
sent two men to him and urged him, "Please come at once!"*

*Peter went with them, and when he arrived he was taken upstairs
to the room. All the widows stood around him, crying
and showing him the robes and other clothing that Dorcas
had made while she was still with them.*

*Peter sent them all out of the room; then he got down on his knees
and prayed. Turning toward the dead woman, he said, "Tabitha, get
up." She opened her eyes, and seeing Peter she sat up. He took her by
the hand and helped her to her feet. Then he called the believers and
the widows and presented her to them alive. This became known all
over Joppa, and many people believed in the Lord.*

ACTS 9:36-42

. . . . ● ● ● ● ● . . . .

THE BOOK OF ACTS holds a unique place in the Bible. It
is a book that clearly shows that the power of this new
kingdom was not for just a privileged few, but for everyone who would believe. And so on the pages of the history of the
birth of the Church, we have the story of Dorcas, a simple woman
of faith, who becomes a marvelous example of faith, humility, and
the power of the risen Christ. Luke's account tells us what occurred
immediately after Christ's ascension to His throne. And in this history, we see how Jesus intended to conduct His government in the

world that He had redeemed by His death. At that time a new, divine power was introduced into human affairs that began to work with tremendous effect in renovating the human race. The power of the Holy Spirit began to turn men and women from the power of sin to righteousness. It is for this reason that the raising of Dorcas to life is of such vital importance in the sacred history. It is one of the seals of the new government, a witness to the power of the new King, whose greatest claim was that He held in His hands the power over life and death.

A Christian community had been formed in the busy seaport of Joppa, no doubt after the pattern of the Mother Church at Jerusalem. Dorcas appears to have been a woman of good social position at Joppa, but her Christian service was not performed in ostentatious ways. She, by the humility of her faith, gave herself wholeheartedly to charitable deeds and the work of her needle. As we will see, she becomes an example of James's ideal of "pure religion and undefiled before God and the Father," which was, "To visit the fatherless and widows in their affliction, and to keep . . . unspotted from the world" (James 1:27, KJV).

Not much is told about Dorcas personally, but what is told contains certain characteristics about her that allow us to conjecture more. Little observations taken in combination often point to a greater significance. And this is the case as we see the kind of woman Dorcas was. She apparently was a lonely woman, but whether she was a single woman or widow, we are not told. If she was a widow, we can imagine how in her loneliness she might, like so many others in the same situation, have grown hard and selfish, or have given way to mourning at the bitterness of her lot in life. But what we read in the text indicates that she did neither. She was a disciple of Jesus and longed to be of use in whatever way she could. And her zeal found an outlet in the "good works," of which, as the sacred historian tells us, she was "full" (v. 36, KJV).

The special charm of Dorcas's acts of kindness to those less fortunate lies in the fact that she worked for the poor with her own hands. She is celebrated for her "good works." Perhaps she remembered her Lord's commendation, "Naked, and ye clothed me" (Matthew 25:36, KJV). If it was true that in clothing the poor she clothed Christ, she would do it with no other hands than her own, for it might be that she would, in spirit at least, draw virtue from the hem of His garments while she made them.

Dorcas was a "woman of a loving heart." It is said that "prosperity gains friends, but adversity tries them." That was not the case with Dorcas. Adversity was to her the sole passport to friendship. The house of Dorcas was a place of refuge for all those in need in Joppa. Wherever need or sickness, poverty or death, were stretching out pale and piteous hands, Dorcas's hand was always ready to grasp them and lift them up. You would have seen her in her little home busy late, working on coats and garments by which she clothed the widows and orphans. Thus, without knowing it, she became a pioneer in Christian work and made herself famous in the Church as the founder of "Dorcas societies."

When Dorcas suddenly died, all of Joppa was shocked. They all believed that she had died way too soon. Isn't it strange that we often don't know the true value of someone until they are no longer with us? Not until then did the apostles of the Church know what a treasure they had had in Dorcas. It soon became apparent that the lonely woman who had faithfully and quietly gone about serving others had won for herself a loving affection from all those who had known her and been blessed by her kind deeds. The widows she had relieved came together to mourn their loss, each sharing how Dorcas seemed able to take each one of them into her heart and make them feel special and cared for. They showed one another all Dorcas's works of love she had made for them. They sent for Peter in their bereavement. It is all a touching, impressive lesson of the abiding influence of a true heart.

The friends of Dorcas probably expected nothing more than Peter's sympathy and counsel at the death of their dear friend. At the same time, they could hardly have failed to hear of the miracle he had just been enabled to work on the paralyzed limbs of Aeneas in Lydda, which was not that far away (Acts 9:32-35). That miracle alone had caused many to come to faith in Lydda and Sharon. Surely the news of it had found its way to the believers in Joppa. They may have nourished a secret hope that even for Dorcas what seemed impossible was possible. At any rate, they sent for Peter, and in the urgency of their need, they said, "Please come at once!" (Acts 9:38) Peter did not hesitate but came immediately.

There are close similarities between the raising of Dorcas and the raising of Jairus's daughter from the dead. Peter had never forgotten that memorable hour, and *now* he knew that he must follow his Lord closely and be led by His Spirit. Before, Peter had been boastful and self-willed and impetuous. He had loved to suggest and dictate and take the lead. But *now,* with all the past graven on his heart, the driving passion of his life was to flow in Jesus' steps and not his own. He knew that death did not have the final claim on a person's life. He had been there when Lazarus had come forth alive from the tomb (John 11:1-44). He had seen the incredulous joy on the faces of Jairus's parents and relatives when Jesus commanded their daughter to come back from death itself (Mark 5:38-43).

Can you imagine the stirring of faith and anticipation going through Peter right then? Not a shadow of doubt or fear could touch him. He knew that the same Spirit that had risen Jesus from the dead was in him and would not fail him in this hour either. And so he thought of all that Jesus had done. Had Jesus asked all the mourners to leave the room? Then Peter must be alone with Dorcas. Had Jesus taken the maiden by the hand and given her back again to her rejoicing friends? Then Peter will present Dorcas alive.

The one point of difference is this: Peter knelt down and *prayed.*

In that one clause lies the difference between the work of Jesus and that of His disciple. For the power of Peter was delegated power. It was Christ who was working, and to Christ he must cry out in faith. But Jesus was acting in His inherent sovereignty. In His own right He is Lord of life and death. He holds the keys of death and hades.

Try to imagine yourself as one of those widows mourning your great loss. In fact, in biblical times there were professional mourners who would stand outside and wail in grief and beat their chests in despair. Today, the visitation hours of most funeral homes have a strained silence hovering over everyone as people gather to pay their respects. A silent hug, whispered words of comfort, handshakes, tears. By no means was it quiet and hushed with those outside of Dorcas's home. There probably was a great number of people gathered outside crying and wailing together.

Then suddenly the door opened and Peter stepped out. He called all the believers and widows together, then presented Dorcas to them alive! Absolute shock rippled through the whole crowd and left them stunned. The believers rejoiced, and many of the others came to faith at that very instant. Just as it had happened in Lydda, the miracle had a profound effect around all of Joppa, for the Word of God says, "This became known all over Joppa, and many people believed in the Lord" (Acts 9:42).

By raising Dorcas from the dead, God meant to set a mark of honor on the love that was displayed. I think this miracle is a demonstration of how impartial His great love is for everyone. Certainly, He would guard the Church against undue estimation of preaching, apostles, miracle-working, deeds of show, gifts, and teach us that beyond all that is His unfathomable love. So He singles out not an apostle, not a martyr, but this gentle, kind woman and crowns her with grandeur and glory, makes her a conqueror of death, and encircles her with a halo of most wonderful, divine, loving care.

LIFE LESSON

· · · · · · · · · · · · · · · · · · ● ● ● · · · · · · · · · · · · · · · · · · ·

Dorcas's life of humble servitude is an example of a woman who took the simple talents she had and by faith and obedience multiplied them to the blessing and benefit of others in need. She forgot about herself and obeyed her Master's teaching to minister to those who were not so fortunate. And when death prematurely claimed her life, she did not go unnoticed by those who loved her. Her rising from the dead at the command of Peter is a confirmation of Jesus' promise, "I am the resurrection and the life" (John 11:25). No matter where you serve the Master, it does not go unnoticed by Him. And no matter how death has touched you, He is still your life.

JAMES HASTINGS

THE DYING THIEF

The Nobody Who Changed His Mind
in the Nick of Time

One of the criminals who hung there hurled insults at him:
"Aren't you the Christ? Save yourself and us!"

But the other criminal rebuked him. "Don't you fear God,"
he said, "since you are under the same sentence? We are punished
justly, for we are getting what our deeds deserve. But this man
has done nothing wrong."

Then he said, "Jesus, remember me when you come into your kingdom."

Jesus answered him, "I tell you the truth,
today you will be with me in paradise."

LUKE 23:39-43

. . . . ● ● ● ● . . . .

O
H, WHAT LESSONS the Gospel of Luke gives us from a nameless man's dying lips. No greater example of Jesus' saving grace can be displayed than to see a common thief, the outcast of society condemned to die, come to faith at the brink of death's door. To those gathered around he is an absolute nobody deserving of his cruel fate, but to Jesus he is the very reason He is hanging on the cross.

A great many people, whenever they hear of the conversion of the dying thief, remember that he was saved from the very clutches of death. He has always been quoted as a case of salvation at the eleventh hour: and so, indeed, he is. His conversion proves that as long as a person can repent, they can obtain forgiveness. The cross of Christ avails even for a man hanging on a cross, and drawing near to his last hour. He who is mighty to save was mighty, even during His own death, to pluck others from the grasp of the destroyer, though they were in the very act of dying.

But that is not everything this story teaches us. And it is a pity to look exclusively at one point, and thus to miss everything else—perhaps miss that which is more important. I do not think that the only uniqueness about the thief is the lateness of his repentance.

First, I think you ought to notice very carefully *the singularity and specialty of the means by which the thief was converted.* The man was an unconverted, impenitent thief when they nailed him to the cross, because Matthew's Gospel says, "In the same way the robbers who were crucified with him also heaped insults on him" (Matthew 27:44). It would appear that by some means or other this thief must have been converted while he was on the cross, for according to Matthew's account, he was hurling insults on Jesus with the rest of those present at the crucifixion.

Nobody preached a sermon to him, and no meeting was held for special prayer on his account. And yet this man became a sincere and accepted believer in the Lord Jesus Christ. What do you think must have converted this poor thief? It must have been the sight of our great Lord and Savior. There was, to begin with, our Savior's amazing behavior on the road to the cross. Not one word of reviling or complaint escaped His lips. Perhaps the robber had been mixed up with all sorts of society, but he had never seen a Man like Jesus. Never had a cross been carried by a Cross-Bearer of His look and manner.

When the thief began to think, in his death pangs, of the singular look of pity that Jesus cast on the women mourning Him, and of the self-forgetfulness that gleamed from His eyes, he must have been struck with wonder. Suddenly, he was smitten with a strange relenting. It was as if an angel had crossed his path and opened his eyes to a new world, and to a new form of manhood, the likes of which he had never seen before.

He and his companion were coarse, rough fellows, but this Jesus was a Man of superior order to any other of the sons of men, for He was the very Son of Man. And when the executioners drove the nails into His hands and feet, this crucified criminal was startled and astonished as he heard Him say, "Father, forgive them, for they do not know what they are doing" (Luke 23:34). It astounded him to hear Jesus pray for His murderers. That was a petition the like of which he had never heard, nor even dreamed of.

And when the cross was lifted up, that thief looked around and could see that inscription written in three languages—"Jesus of Nazareth, the King of the Jews." Putting this and that together—that strange Person, incarnate loveliness, all patience and majesty, that strange prayer of forgiveness, and now this singular inscription—this poor thief began to have a ray of hope dawn on his heart. Surely he who knew the Old Testament prophecies said to himself, "Is this truly the King of the Jews? Is He who wrought miracles and raised the dead, and said that He was the Son of God really our Messiah?"

As the dying thief watched, he heard people shout, "He saved others. Can't he save himself." Even the very words of disdain hurled at Jesus from those who crucified Him became the gospel to this poor dying thief. Perhaps this man learned the gospel from those who jested at our dying Lord. And so the servants of the devil were unconsciously made to be the servants of Christ.

But now consider the *uniqueness of this man's faith*. This man believed in Christ when he literally saw Him dying the death of a felon, enduring the greatest possible personal shame as He hung on that cross. For him to ask Jesus to remember him when He came into His kingdom, though he saw Jesus bleeding His life away, and hounded to the death, was a splendid act of trust. For him to commit his everlasting destiny into the hands of One who was, to all appearance, unable even to preserve His own life, was a noble achievement of faith. What he saw was more to his hindrance rather than to his help, for he saw Jesus in the very extremity of agony and death, and yet he believed in Him as the King shortly to come to His kingdom. He saw so much, though his eyes of faith had been opened for so short a time!

And *consider the result of his faith.* This dying thief first of all confessed the Lord Jesus Christ, and that is the very essence of baptism. Did he not also acknowledge Him to his fellow thief and rebuke him? It was as public a confession as he could possibly make. The apostle Paul says, "That if you confess with your mouth, 'Jesus is Lord,' and believe in your heart that God raised him from the dead, you will be saved" (Romans 10:9). The very least thing that the Lord Jesus Christ can expect of us is that we confess Him to the best of our power. This man came out, then and there, and made as open an avowal of his faith in Christ as was possible.

The next thing he did was to rebuke his fellow sinner. He spoke to him in answer to the vile words with which he had assailed the Lord. Do you not know that a person who is silent when a wrong thing is said or done may become a participator in the sin?

Then the dying thief made a full confession of his guilt. He said to him who was crucified with him, " 'Don't you fear God . . . since you are under the same sentence? We are punished justly, for we are getting what our deeds deserve. But this man has done nothing wrong' " (Luke 23:40-41). When a man is willing to confess that he deserves the wrath of God—that he deserves the suffering that his sin has brought upon him—there is evidence of sincerity in him. In this man's case, his repentance glittered like a holy tear in the eye of his faith, so that his faith was covered with the drops of his penitence.

He *adored and worshipped Jesus,* for he said, "Jesus, remember me when you come into your kingdom" (Luke 23:42). And then the Lord gracefully in His darkest hour bestowed a promise to this man's singular eye of faith, "I tell you the truth, today you will be with me in paradise" (Luke 23:43).

This nameless robber breakfasted with the devil, but he dined with Christ on earth, and supped with Him in Paradise. Why is it that our Lord does not take us all to Paradise? It is because He has something for us to do here. May the Spirit of God make something of us yet, so that we may go as diligent servants from the labors of the vineyard to the pleasures of Paradise.

LIFE LESSON

· · · · · · · · · · · · · · · · ● ● ● · · · · · · · · · · · · · · · ·

Whether you are at the earliest stage of life, or are within a few hours of eternity, if you fly for refuge to the hope set before you in the gospel of our Lord Jesus Christ, you will be saved. No matter what sin has enslaved you for years, the gospel excludes none on the grounds of age or character. You must only look away from your sin in repentance and "believe on the Lord Jesus Christ, and you will be saved." That is the message the Holy Spirit yearns to whisper to every heart. "Now is the time of God's favor, now is the day of salvation" (2 Corinthians 6:2).

CHARLES SPURGEON

ELIEZER
of DAMASCUS

The Nobody Who Nearly Won the Powerball Lotto

*But Abram said, "O Sovereign LORD, what can you give me
since I remain childless and the one who will inherit my estate
is Eliezer of Damascus?" And Abram said, "You have given me
no children; so a servant in my household will be my heir."*

GENESIS 15:2-3

· · · · · · · · · · · · · · · · · · ● · ● · ● · · · · · · · · · · · · · · · · ·

WHO WAS THIS ELIEZER OF DAMASCUS, and how is
it that a mere servant stands to inherit the vast wealth
and possessions of one so great as Abraham? Or,
should we ask, how is it that a mere *slave*, for in this biblical context a servant is but a mild way of saying slave, should find himself
in the fortunate position of being in line for Abraham's inheritance? How does one from a class so often utterly despised by the
world become so highly honored both by Abraham as well as God?

Given his role as a slave as well as the riches being directed his
way, one might think that Eliezer of Damascus played the Fertile
Crescent Powerball Lotto and was holding the only winning ticket.

While it is not clear how or when Eliezer became a part of
Abraham's household, the hard fact remains that he was a slave. At
one point in time Abraham had over three hundred men at his disposal who were trained slaves (Genesis 14:14), indicating well over
a thousand servants in his ownership. While it appears that
Abraham ruled his household with a gentle hand as one who was
not afraid to stand before God and be accountable for his actions,
Eliezer was locked in a system of human bondage.

Although Eliezer was a slave, he had risen to the highest place in his master's service—the one in whom Abraham had complete confidence in all the important matters of his household. His situation appears similar to that of Joseph when he was enslaved in Potiphar's house (Genesis 39). It was not uncommon for one who had been sold or born into slavery to rise in the changes of fortune from the bottom of servitude to the very top. But the fact that Eliezer had been specified as Abraham's sole heir raises the bar far higher than the finest servant could ever dream of.

Eliezer possessed an unlimited reservoir of the one key dynamic found in successful servanthood—unswerving faithfulness. His was the truthfulness that would never resort to a lie. His was an honesty that refused to cheat or swindle, even though he had opportunity after opportunity to take advantage of his access to Abraham's funds. He epitomized the meaning of a word that is seldom used today unless someone is referring to mutual funds—Eliezer was a man of *fidelity*.

Eliezer's was a single eye to his master's interests at every point. He was as hardworking and responsible when out of Abraham's sight as when he was in it. Eliezer did not do things behind his master's back that he would not do in his presence. The very long period during which Eliezer held this important office in Abraham's house is proof of this. Only by trustworthiness can such a position be kept, and Eliezer served in his role for at least fifty years. He was Abraham's steward before Isaac was born, and still steward when Isaac married—two events separated by nearly half a century.

To comprehend Eliezer's fidelity, one must recall what the birth of Isaac meant to Eliezer. Though it was the wonderful fulfillment of God's promise to Abraham and Sarah, and an epic event as regards the history of the world, it was far otherwise for Eliezer, at least from a worldly point of view. From all appearances, had Abraham died without an heir, he intended to bypass his nephew

Lot as well as his relatives in Mesopotamia and give his entire estate to the faithful Eliezer. The unprecedented prospect of moving from slavery to freedom as well as staggering wealth vanished like smoke at the birth of Isaac.

Perhaps Eliezer still held to the slender hope that the beloved son might never marry, leaving no heir behind? Even this expectation, if he ever cherished it, was also to be extinguished in a rather dramatic fashion. Surely it was no small challenge to Eliezer's faithfulness when Abraham commissioned him to seek a wife for Isaac! Eliezer had to quench his own hope of rising in the world if he was to remain true to his master. That Abraham believed Eliezer of Damascus would be loyal despite the severity of the conflict of interests is amazing.

If you read the full account of Eliezer's story in Genesis 24, you see how Abraham's confidence in Eliezer was justified. Handed the daunting responsibility of finding a wife worthy of Isaac from among Abraham's relatives in his distant homeland, Eliezer also must convince the young woman to return with him. All the plans were left to him alone. Wisely, he selected some costly jewelry and splendid articles of clothing for presents. And Eliezer took ten camels and a group of men, which indicated both the rank of his master and the importance of his mission. This faithful servant, Eliezer of Damascus, then kissed away all his own personal hopes of greatness and set out on the four hundred-mile journey for Mesopotamia.

Brown with the desert's dust, and scorched by the heat, and worn out with the labors of the long journey, Eliezer finally arrived within sight of the city where Nahor, the elder brother of Abraham, lived. It was at the time of day when the women of the city came to the wells to draw water. He immediately committed his objective to God, praying, "O LORD, God of my master Abraham, give me success today, and show kindness to my master Abraham.... May it be that when I say to a girl, 'Please let down your jar that I may have a drink,' and she says, 'Drink, and I'll water your camels too'— let her be the one you have chosen for your servant Isaac. By this I will know that you have shown kindness to my master" (vv. 12-14).

What a remarkable, noble regard to his master imbues this prayer of Eliezer, and what wisdom in seeking a wife for Isaac who must demonstrate herself to be humble, courteous, hardworking, and kind. And what faith to believe that any woman would be willing to draw gallons upon gallons of water for ten thirsty camels and a bunch of tired men she didn't know!

"Before he had finished praying," the answer came in the form of Rebekah (v. 15). She was both very beautiful and a virgin, and her gracious reply to Eliezer's request for water hit the mark of his prayer. Even then, while she was drawing water for all ten camels, "without saying a word, the man watched her closely to learn whether or not the LORD had made his journey successful" (v. 21). What a remarkable man of character Eliezer was! He must be certain beyond a shadow of a doubt that Rebekah was God's answer.

The clincher comes when he finally asks her name and discovers that she is Nahor's daughter. He is so thrilled that he bows to worship God, saying, "Praise be to the LORD, the God of my master Abraham, who has not abandoned his kindness and faithfulness to my master. As for me, the LORD has led me on the journey to the house of my master's relatives" (v. 27). It's hard to imagine his prayer being answered in a clearer way.

Even still, he moves quickly beyond the answered prayer and seeks to win Rebekah's heart as well as the heart of her family, refusing to stop to eat or be refreshed from his journey until he has fulfilled his duties. Talk about a deal closer! When given a task to accomplish, this is a man who never quits until it's done, and he does it with all his strength. Before considering any of his own comforts, he must tell his story and mission and get a commitment. And once he has that commitment, he allows but one day's rest before insisting that they return to Abraham. Eliezer will not allow anything to delay the success that God has granted all along the route (v. 56).

End of story. Rebekah packed her bags and hopped on the next camel headed southwest with Eliezer. She took one look at Isaac and fell in love, and the two of them lived happily ever after (well, not quite). Abraham died in peace, and good old Eliezer is not heard from again. His biggest assignment completed and monumentally successful, we are left to wonder if Abraham gave him his freedom.

Whether a free man or a slave, Eliezer was an outstanding man of prayer and service. His confidence in the faithfulness and providence of God was extraordinary. What was said concerning Abraham, "Abram believed the LORD, and he credited it to him as righteousness" (Genesis 15:6), is unmistakably reflected in the life of Eliezer. With the first indication of success, he bowed his head and worshiped in gratitude. The saying, *Like master like man*, has never found a more appropriate illustration.

LIFE LESSON

Eliezer of Damascus, perhaps more than any other servant in all of history, fulfilled the high calling given to slaves by the apostle Paul: "Teach slaves to be subject to their masters in everything, to try to please them, not to talk back to them, and not to steal from them, but to show that they can be fully trusted, so that in every way they will make the teaching about God our Savior attractive" (Titus 2:9-10). We may not be enslaved as Eliezer was, but we are servants of Jesus Christ whose one mission in life was to do the will of His Father in heaven. Through humility and service we are called to be living epistles of Jesus Christ, seen and read by all men, to live as to recommend His truth and ways to the admiration and love of others.

THOMAS GUTHRIE

THE ETHIOPIAN EUNUCH

The Nobody Who Couldn't Wait to Get Dunked

*Now an angel of the Lord said to Philip, "Go south to the road—
the desert road—that goes down from Jerusalem to Gaza."
So he started out, and on his way he met an Ethiopian eunuch,
an important official in charge of all the treasury of Candace,
queen of the Ethiopians. This man had gone to Jerusalem to worship,
and on his way home was sitting in his chariot reading the book
of Isaiah the prophet. The Spirit told Philip,
"Go to that chariot and stay near it."*

ACTS 8:26-29

. . . . ● ● ● ● . . . .

O N THE DAY THAT STEPHEN was stoned to death because of his courageous speech to the Sanhedrin, the Bible says "a great persecution broke out against the church at Jerusalem, and all except the apostles were scattered throughout Judea and Samaria" (Acts 8:1). At the same time, we also read that "Saul began to destroy the church. Going from house to house, he dragged off men and women and put them in prison" (v. 3). Those who were scattered throughout Judea and Samaria began to preach the Word wherever they went (v. 4). It was the very beginning of the fulfillment of the word spoken by Jesus, "You will be my witnesses in Jerusalem, and in all Judea and Samaria" (Acts 1:8).

Philip left Jerusalem and went down to a city in Samaria and preached the message of Jesus there. And the power of the Holy Spirit confirmed Philip's word with miraculous signs. Because of those demonstrations of power, "they all paid close attention to what he said" (Acts 8:6). The gospel had such a tremendous effect in that area that soon word of those coming to faith reached Jerusalem. The text says that "when the apostles in Jerusalem heard that Samaria had accepted the word of God, they sent Peter and John to them" (Acts 8:14). Now the amazing shock is that the Word was producing tremendous fruit among the Samaritans—people the Jews normally would not even associate with. But God's free grace has no social boundaries or restrictions. Jesus had died for all, even the Samaritans. And so Peter and John came from Jerusalem and prayed for these believers that they might receive the Holy Spirit (Acts 8:14). The evidence of God's working was so great that Peter and John preached the gospel in many Samaritan villages on their return trip to Jerusalem.

It was during this great outpouring of the Spirit of God that we find Philip given a specific direction "by an angel of the Lord" (v. 26). To understand this radical new direction God had given him, let's put it into some perspective. Picture Billy Graham, perhaps the greatest evangelist of all time, suddenly turning from a great ministry to go to some obscure place to share the good news of Jesus with one person and then going on to something different after that. That's exactly what we find Philip doing when the Spirit directs him to leave Samaria and go south on a desert road toward Gaza. To man's reasoning, it probably seemed a bit strange for Philip to leave such a great revival. Yet as the prophet Isaiah said, "As the heavens are higher than the earth, so are my ways higher than your ways and my thoughts than your thoughts" (Isaiah 55:9).

One of the greatest ways to see God move in our lives is to imitate the same obedience Philip demonstrated whenever God spoke to him. The Book of Acts is full of instances where people obey God, and as a result, the gospel is spread farther and farther into the Gentile world. Undoubtedly, there were people who wanted Philip to stay and continue the work where all the miraculous signs were happening. But God had a bigger plan that would carry the gospel all the way to Africa. As Philip travels along this desert road, he happens upon an Ethiopian eunuch riding in his chariot. Now this Ethiopian wasn't just your common traveler on the road. He may have been a nobody to most Israelites, but he was an "important official in charge of all the treasury of Candace, queen of the Ethiopians" (v. 27). He was a man of position and influence.

And from our text, we learn that he was a proselyte to the faith of Israel and had made a long and perilous journey to Jerusalem to worship (v. 27). We are not told who he met and spent time with, but because of his position and responsibilities within Queen Candace's court, it is safe to assume that he also came to do some business, which would have required letters of introduction. It is very possible that he was directed and recommended to some of the heads of the temple: to Annas, or to Caiaphas, or to some other ecclesiastical dignitary. But whatever his business at the temple or elsewhere, we now see him returning and reading from the prophet Isaiah in his chariot on the very road to where God had sent Philip.

Was the Book of the prophet Isaiah a parting gift from a Jerusalem host to this man on the day of his departure for home? Or was the sacred Book this good eunuch's own selection? We do not know, but reading he was, and he was reading out loud, which was common in those cultures.

All this time Philip is wandering up and down the wilderness road. Do you think he might have wondered if he had mistaken his own imagination for the voice of the Lord? Caravans of pilgrims come and go. Merchants of Egypt and of Arabia and cohorts of Roman soldiers travel the same road. Then in the midst of his wondering why he is on that road, at last, a chariot of distinction comes in sight. When it comes within earshot, Philip hears with the utmost astonishment the master of the chariot reading aloud. Now, he is not astonished at this official reading out loud, but his admiration and amazement are unbounded when he hears *what* the Ethiopian is reading: "He was led like a sheep to the slaughter, and as a lamb before the shearer is silent, so he did not open his mouth. In his humiliation he was deprived of justice. Who can speak of his descendants? For his life was taken from the earth" (Acts 8:32-33).

Was it the eunuch's own serious instincts that led him to those particular verses in Isaiah? (And remember, chapter and verse numbers were not part of the scroll he was reading at that time.) Or had he heard that profound and perplexing passage disputed over in one of the synagogues of Jerusalem? We do not know. Only, it is remarkable that out of the whole Old Testament this utter stranger to the Old Testament was pondering over its most central chapter, and its most profound prophecy, as he rode in his chariot.

By God's providential wisdom, Philip was there to ask the simple question, "Do you understand what you are reading?" (v. 30) The eunuch responded humbly, "How can I . . . unless someone explains it to me?" (v. 31) And he invited Philip to join him. Don't you think that Philip was probably chuckling to himself at how this had worked out? It was also a confirmation to him of correctly discerning the Lord's direction. Philip must have marveled at the "divine encounter," for by now he understood the Lord's wisdom in bringing him there. So he joined the Ethiopian in his chariot and began to tell him all the good news about Jesus: who He was, and what He had done to fulfill the very prophecy the man had been reading. God says that a humble heart is precious in His sight, and it is by humility that we receive His wisdom and the opening of our understanding (Proverbs 11:2). And that is exactly what this Ethiopian did. He believed the word that Philip spoke to him. It is obvious that Philip had spoken of being baptized, because when they came upon some water, the Ethiopian said, "Look, here is water. Why shouldn't I be baptized?" (v. 36) His heart believed and he was baptized right there along the desert road.

When he was baptized, "the Spirit of the Lord suddenly took Philip away, and the eunuch did not see him again, but went on his way rejoicing" (v. 39). God's timing was perfect. He placed Philip at the right place to witness to a man who held a high position back in the Ethiopian court. Upon his return, we can rest assured that he would have shared the gospel he had just received with those around him. Only eternity will tell of those who will be among the throngs who worship the Lamb because of this one's man conversion on a lonely road in the wilderness.

LIFE LESSON

· · · · · · · · · · · · · · · · ● ● ● · · · · · · · · · · · · · · · ·

As you walk in the newness of life you have in Christ, always be open to the direction of the Holy Spirit. There will be times when you will be caught up in some of the great movings of the Spirit. Those are times that bring great rejoicing! But let your walk with God be sensitive to His voice, for Jesus said that His sheep know His voice (John 10:27). And when you least expect it, He will direct you somewhere to talk to someone you never would have talked to on your own. That person— like the Ethiopian—will have a sphere of influence where their conversion will have an effect like the ripples of a stone tossed into a still pond. And even more people will hear of the good news in Jesus and come to faith because of your obedience.

ALEXANDER WHYTE

EZEKIEL'S WIFE

The Nobody Who Was a Delight to Her Husband

*The word of the LORD came to me: "Son of man, with one blow
I am about to take away from you the delight of your eyes.
Yet do not lament or weep or shed any tears. Groan quietly;
do not mourn for the dead. Keep your turban fastened
and your sandals on your feet; do not cover the lower part
of your face or eat the customary food of mourners."*

*So I spoke to the people in the morning, and in the evening
my wife died. The next morning I did as I had been commanded.*

EZEKIEL 24:15-18

THE YEAR WAS 586 B.C., and these were dark days for the
Jewish people. The prophet Ezekiel was among the Jewish
exiles by the river Chebar, which is thought to have been
the royal canal of the Babylonian king Nebuchadnezzar, the *Nahr
Malcha*, which connected the Tigris and Euphrates. The Jewish
captives were probably employed in the excavation of this great
canal in Mesopotamia. Ezekiel was trying to bring home to his people's hearts and consciences the calamities that threatened their
beloved city of Jerusalem. The besieging army of Nebuchadnezzar
had surrounded it, and the word of God had gone out that
Jerusalem and the Kingdom of Judah should fall. It might seem
that the prophet could convince the people of this fact without any
visual sign, and certainly without a sign that would devastate the
heart of the prophet. But the divine wisdom thought otherwise.

This moving tragedy in the prophet's life was to convey unmistakable facts and lessons to the people of the captivity. Ezekiel had
a wife whom he loved tenderly. And the word of Yahweh came to

him that she would die on that very day, and he must not mourn. So he spent the whole morning fulfilling his prophetic tasks, and the people could not help taking notice, for his tones were ravishing in their sweetness and his actions were curious in their symbolism. Did he return from his morning labors for a few hours of conversation with the beloved woman who would die that very night? Did he talk with her regarding it? What would any of us do if put in such a position?

All the captive Jewish community by the Chebar would hear of her death in the evening, and they would gather in the morning to inquire and comfort. Friends would bring the provisions for the funeral feast, which were the usual means of consoling the bereaved (Jeremiah 16:5-7). Enemies—not everyone appreciated the hard truths that Ezekiel spoke—might also come by to point out the perceived moral: "Now, prophet, who has prophesied the ruin of your own people, see, Yahweh has brought the same sorrow on you instead." For it could not be hid from anyone that this wife was the desire of Ezekiel's eyes, his one comforter and companion, his one light and joy in the thankless task of his isolated prophetic life far from Jerusalem.

But the people found Ezekiel in the morning without any of the customary signs of mourning. No tears marked his face. His hair was not tousled; his feet were not bare. There were no preparations under way for the funeral banquet. His face was firm and set; his voice did not tremble. The sight of this passionless grief aroused their curiosity. What could it mean? Even a husband who did not love his wife would mourn for appearance sake. Yet, here was one who was known to love his wife passionately, and he did not shed a tear?

The whole community gathered to learn the meaning of Ezekiel's strange actions, which they felt at once to be a sign from God. His reply was immediate and incisive (Ezekiel 24:20-27). He was indeed a sign to them of their approaching experience. Their own decisive doom soon to come. Their holy temple in Jerusalem was being burned with fire; their sons and daughters were being slain. In a word, they were losing the desire of their eyes; and their astonished grief would not permit the usual signs of mourning.

That was the immediate message, but it suggested more. Through the personal experience of His prophet Ezekiel, God would bring home in the most touching way the anguish in His own heart over the destruction of the city He had chosen. And perhaps, though we tread on more visionary ground, He would suggest by the undying love of a bereaved husband and the dim conviction of a restoration to his wife that the separation between Himself and His people would not be forever, but would end in a future restoration.

LIFE LESSON

. . . . ● ● ● . . . .

None of us are spared from life's deepest sorrows. Not even the greatest of prophets and biblical saints, not even our Savior Jesus Christ, was spared from the pain and grief of death. But thank God that death has already been defeated by the death of Jesus Christ on the cross. Death's bitter sting has been removed, and on a day that has yet to come, it will be utterly destroyed. God will wipe away every tear from our eyes, and death shall be no more, neither shall there be mourning nor crying nor pain anymore. Let us live in this glorious hope.

J. G. GREENHOUGH

GOMER, the WIFE of HOSEA

The Nobody Who Was Nearly Unlovable

*When the LORD began to speak through Hosea, the LORD
said to him, "Go, take to yourself an adulterous wife and children
of unfaithfulness, because the land is guilty of the vilest adultery in
departing from the LORD." So he married Gomer daughter of
Diblaim, and she conceived and bore him a son.*

HOSEA 1:2-3

HOSEA THE PROPHET'S MINISTRY encompasses the tragic last days of the northern kingdom of Israel, during which six kings, all rotten to the core, reigned within twenty-five years. Both Hosea and the prophet Amos tell us that it was a period of material wealth, shameless luxury, and pitiless oppression of the poor. It was a time of spiritual decline and apostasy, and it was the prophet's unhappy task to denounce the coming fall of the reigning house of Jehu. These were extraordinarily difficult days to be a messenger of God to His wayward people.

From his writings, it is clear that Hosea was a man of tender feeling, born to be a devoted husband and father, a patriot and lover of his people. He was the antithesis of all the evil going on around him. While it was his stern duty to chastise the land he loved, he tried to win it to repentance by passionate appeals. And as a national object lesson, he was directed by God to marry Gomer. All his public ministry is simply a spiritual application of the life that he lived with her, and it came at a great cost to his soul.

Gomer was a high-class prostitute, and, as strange as it seems to us, Hosea sought her in marriage for that very reason. In the luxurious Court of Samaria, she was distinguished as a courtesan, which is a fancy word for a mistress associated with the rich and powerful who provided her with all the seductive attractions and luxuries that went with it. The scandal that would result by Hosea's marriage to her was precisely what the prophet desired. By this he expected to gain the attention of the king and the court and the nation.

It must have been an indescribable cross for Hosea to bring such a woman to his home. But if we are to follow the indications of his book (2:14 and other places), we must conclude that she entirely won his heart, and her irrepressible unfaithfulness broke the heart that she had won. The pathos and tragedy of his writing—which make his book the most moving Old Testament presentation of God's yearning love over His rebellious people—are all drawn from the experience of his own heart's longing for the loyalty of Gomer.

If it were possible to gaze into the heart of Gomer, what might we find? At the birth of her first son, she could not conceal the meaning of the name Hosea gave him (1:4). "Jezreel" was an explicit sign that the vengeance of God was coming on King Jeroboam for the treatment of Jezreel (2 Kings 10:1-14). Whether she liked it or not, Gomer found herself engaged in a prophetic mission. And in her lewd ways and despicable treatment of her husband, every corrupt Israelite was compelled to see a picture of his own country and of his own heart lived out before them. The message was unmistakable.

This love of Hosea did not fail, but renewed itself. And in due course, Gomer bore Hosea a daughter. Again the prophetic will appointed the name (1:6). "Lo-Ruhamah" means "not loved" or "not pitied"—that is, the land of Israel was passing beyond the reach of even the mercy of God. Its doom was rapidly being sealed. Does not some solemnity creep even into the heart of Gomer? It is one thing to hear the message from God; it is another thing to participate in the delivery of that somber word.

And when her third child came and was given the name,

"Lo-Ammi," which means "not my people," surely she and her old friends must have trembled at the prophetic meaning. If they did not tremble, they should have. Nevertheless, after three years of being loved by Hosea and at least outwardly being the prophet's wife, Gomer broke away and returned to her old life of shame.

If you read through Hosea's second chapter, you have to wonder if his words of pleading actually went from the deserted husband through her children, who were now old enough to talk? Did his son Jezreel lead his little sister and brother to Gomer's house and say to her, "This little one is now called My People, and we call our sister Pitied"? Did the three children speak to her of how Hosea spoke of her in loving terms, how he cried in his sorrow that she was not his wife, and then called out to her in pitiful terms of desire?

And then chapter three makes sense. The woman referred to is the beloved but erring Gomer, the very symbol of the sinful nation. And Yahweh's compassion and unfailing purpose to save are expressed in what now takes place. It appears that both Gomer's youth and beauty have gone, and she is no longer in favor at the king's court. She has been reduced to a mere woman of the town, open to every chance comer. Once she had been sought by the rich, who gave her abundance (2:5), but now a few shekels of silver and a few bushels of barley appear as riches (3:2). Her painted face only provokes ridicule, and the awful doom of those who prostitute love sets in upon her.

Embittered, Gomer is left with nothing to hope for, except to wait for a hideous end. But who is this upon her doorstep? Miracle of forgiveness and compassion, it is her husband Hosea who has come to claim her. With a grave irony, he offers her money and food as her hire. And with strange prophetic meaning, he tells her that she must now be his wife at last, since all others have turned from her. The man whom she has most deeply wounded is the only one who can forgive, the only one who cares. We can only hope that she responded and finally came home.

LIFE LESSON

. . . . ● ● ● . . . .

If you find Hosea's love amazing, which it truly is, consider that *God is love* (1 John 4:8). There is nothing more important for you than to know and respond to His love in the depths of your heart. The great King Solomon said that he denied himself no pleasure and took delight in all his work only to find that it all was meaningless, a chasing after the wind (Ecclesiastes 1:14). No one whose heart has been captured by the love of God need ever echo such hollow sentiments.

ROBERT HORTON

THE GRATEFUL LEPER

The Nobody Who Remembered His Manners

Now on his way to Jerusalem, Jesus traveled along the border between Samaria and Galilee. As he was going into a village, ten men who had leprosy met him. They stood at a distance and called out in a loud voice, "Jesus, Master, have pity on us!"

When he saw them, he said, "Go, show yourselves to the priests." And as they went, they were cleansed.

One of them, when he saw he was healed, came back, praising God in a loud voice. He threw himself at Jesus' feet and thanked him— and he was a Samaritan.

Jesus asked, "Were not all ten cleansed? Where are the other nine? Was no one found to return and give praise to God except this foreigner?" Then he said to him, "Rise and go; your faith has made you well."

LUKE 17:11-19

. . . . ● ● ● ● . . . .

THE MELANCHOLY GROUP of outcast lepers that Jesus met in one of the villages on the borders of Samaria and Galilee on His way to Jerusalem was made up of Samaritans and Jews. The common misery of their dreaded disease drove them together, in spite of racial hatred, because the only people they could be around were other lepers. People who suffered from leprosy were forbidden by the Law of Moses to live with those who did not have the disease. They were treated as untouchables and lived a lonely life of rejection. Perhaps these Bible nobodies had met in order to appeal to Jesus, thinking to move Him by their combined wretchedness.

They stood afar off from others, and the distance prescribed by the Law forced them to cry aloud, though it must have been an effort, for one symptom of leprosy is a hoarse whisper. But a desperate need can often momentarily give a person strange physical power. Their cry indicates that they had some knowledge of who Jesus was. They knew the Lord's name and had some notions of His authority, for they addressed Him as Jesus and as Master. They also knew that He had the power to heal, and they hoped that He had mercy, which they might win for themselves by their combined plea for His help. The tiny seed of trust is seen in their desperate cry. But their conceptions of Him, and their consciousness of their own necessities, did not rise above the purely physical realm, and He was nothing more to them than a healer who had gained some fame.

Their faltering faith and the cry for mercy moved Jesus to compassion, and when He saw them, He said, "Go, show yourselves to the priests" (v. 14). He went toward them, but in this instance of healing, He did not touch them. The command He gave them recognized and honored the requirements of the Law. His main purpose, no doubt, was to test, and thereby to strengthen, the lepers' trust. He simply told them to go and show themselves to the priest, for to be restored to society, the Law of Moses required the priest pronounce healing so that everyone would know and believe the person was truly clean (Leviticus 13:45-46).

To set out to go to the priest while they still felt themselves full of leprosy would have seemed absolutely absurd, unless they believed that Jesus could and would heal them. He did not pronounce a healing as he had done to another case of leprosy (Matthew 8:1-14). Instead, He told them to go in faith and present themselves to the priest. And as they obeyed His Word, Luke records the event for us, saying, "And as they went, they were cleansed" (v. 14). The healing was granted to them as they stepped out and obeyed in faith. The whole ten set off at once. They had received all they wanted from the Lord and had no more thought about Him. So they turned their backs on Him.

Leprosy is a hideous disease that robs people of the sense of feeling as the nerves lose their ability to function. Imagine what it must have felt for them to actually feel the healing taking place in their bodies as they ran off in haste to find a priest. How much more confidently they must have picked up the pace as the glow of returning health surged new life through their bodies. The cure is a remarkable demonstration of Christ's power, for it is performed at a distance, without even a word. It is simply the silent working of His power. It is a good reminder that when we bring what may seem a hopeless case to Jesus, we may have to set out in faith as those lepers did even while we still feel the particular "leprosy" that is plaguing us.

Yet Luke tells us that "one of them, when he saw he was healed, came back, praising God in a loud voice. He threw himself at Jesus' feet and thanked him—and he was a Samaritan" (vv. 15-16). The nine might have said, "We are doing what the Healer commanded us to do. To go back to Him would be disobedience." But a grateful heart knows that to express its gratitude is the highest duty and is necessary for its own relief. The voice of this one leper that had to, possibly for years, cry out a warning to stay away now lost all inhibition and in adoration kneeled before Jesus and shouted his thanks in a loud voice. True gratitude of the soul will always praise God with a thankful spirit, for it knows that its deliverance has not come from the hand of man, but from God's hand of mercy and compassion.

This leper's voice was very different now from the strained croak of his earlier request for healing. He knew that he had two to thank—God and Jesus. Thankfulness knits us to Jesus with a blessed bond. Nothing is so sweet to a loving heart than to pour itself out in thanks to Him who touches our diseased soul and body.

"And he was a Samaritan" (v. 16). That may be Luke's main reason for telling the story. It is a poignant reminder that in Jesus' ministry to people, the common human virtues were often found abundantly in individuals against whom the Jews were deeply prejudiced. We also see a side of Christ by His question to the leper who had returned to give thanks, "Were not all ten cleansed? Where are the other nine? Was no one found to return and give praise to God except this foreigner?" (v. 17) Note Jesus' sad wonder at man's ingratitude and yet at the same time a joyful recognition of a foreigner's thankfulness.

We increase the deep appreciation of our gifts by our thankfulness for them. We taste them twice, as it were, when we open our mouths and express our gratitude in praise with a loud voice. Jesus rejoiced over this unknown Samaritan and gave him a greater gift than he had received when the leprosy was cleared from his flesh. The Revised Version margin reads, "saved thee." Surely we may take that word in its deepest meaning and believe that a more fatal leprosy melted out of this man's spirit. The faith that had begun in a confidence that Jesus could heal, and had been increased by obedience to the command that tried it, and had become more awed by the experience of bodily healing, and been deepened by finding a tongue to express itself in thankfulness, now rose to a comprehenion of who Jesus was and resulted in a salvation that healed his spirit as well as his body.

LIFE LESSON

· ● ● ● ● ·

If you want a key to growing in your Christian life, then learn the lesson of gratitude that this leper has taught us. Are we like the other nine lepers who receive something from God and then hurry off clutching our blessings and never cast back a thought to the Giver? Let us not impoverish ourselves by dishonoring Him by the ingratitude of our hearts. Rather, let us do as the apostle Paul exhorts, "Let the word of Christ dwell in you richly as you teach and admonish one another with all wisdom, and as you sing psalms, hymns and spiritual songs with gratitude in your hearts to God" (Colossians 3:16).

ALEXANDER MACLAREN

HADAD
the EDOMITE

The Nobody Who Loved His Home

*Then the LORD raised up against Solomon an adversary, Hadad the
Edomite, from the royal line of Edom. Earlier when David was fighting with Edom, Joab the commander of the army, who had gone up to
bury the dead, had struck down all the men in Edom. Joab and all
the Israelites stayed there for six months, until they had destroyed all
the men in Edom. But Hadad, still only a boy, fled to Egypt with
some Edomite officials who had served his father. . . . They went to
Egypt, to Pharaoh king of Egypt, who gave Hadad a house and land
and provided him with food.*

*Pharaoh was so pleased with Hadad that he gave him a sister of his
own wife, Queen Tahpenes, in marriage. . . .While he was in Egypt,
Hadad heard that David rested with his fathers and that Joab the
commander of the army was also dead. Then Hadad said to Pharaoh,
"Let me go, that I may return to my own country."*

*"What have you lacked here that you want to go back
to your own country?" Pharaoh asked.*

"Nothing," Hadad replied, "but do let me go!"

1 KINGS 11:14-22

. . . . ● ● ● ● . . . .

H ADAD'S EARLY YEARS had known hard times, bitter
sorrow, and untold tragedy. He had been made a home-
less orphan amid the horror and bloodshed of a merci-
less war of genocide, and driven from his own land as a child, leaving death and desolation behind. In the company of other forlorn
fugitives, he escaped his nation's borders and found his way to Egypt,

where things had gone extraordinarily well for him as a stranger in a new land. While we know little of the circumstances surrounding his arrival, Hadad found unusual favor in the eyes of Pharaoh, who endowed him with rich estates and gave him a princess in marriage. In other words, Hadad struck it rich, leaving behind a vanquished past and becoming Pharaoh's favored brother-in-law.

One would think that Hadad would drift from the biblical screen and not be heard from again. There were a hundred good reasons why he should have settled into his cushy position under the benevolence of Pharaoh and been content with it. Egypt was the wealthiest of countries, the advanced place of culture, civilization, and luxury, while Edom was little more than clusters of barren hills tenanted by ragged shepherds whose futures were not about to become prosperous. Why, asked the generous Pharaoh, could Hadad not be happy with the good fortune? Was he lacking anything? No, replied Hadad, everything possible had been done to give him a royal welcome and great future. There was no substantial reason for leaving except for sentiment. Edom, after all, was his own land—the land of his birth and childhood on which his eyes had opened on golden mornings, the land of friends and the graves of his father and ancestors. Call it a foolish whim if you like, but it was an irresistible desire that drew him back like strong chains.

That is the whole of the story, with no particular spiritual lesson attached to it, at least at first glance. Yet the inspired writers have given this Bible nobody a permanent place in Scripture, and I think it is because the sentiment that it illustrates is beautiful, because the affections for one's own land and people are only less spiritual than one's reverence for God. These sentiments, preferences, and attachments that we cannot explain are often the most powerful of all and form the noblest and richest part of our lives. They have the power to make the stones of Edom preferable to the luxurious courts of Egypt.

Why should the place where you were born and the scenes of your early life possess a peculiar charm above all others? No reason for which you can tell, but a thousand reasons you can feel. Why does a humble house in which you have made a home seem far richer to you than the grandest mansions that belong to others? Why are your spouse and children more to you than all the other families in the world? How is it that a nation can have such a hold upon your heart and soul? You cannot explain these things, yet they are the sweetest of human realities.

I'll tell you what Hadad may have felt as he considered his homeland. Recall your feelings as you witnessed the events of September 11, 2001, and try to put your feelings of patriotism and national concern in perspective. There is something spiritual in them, there is a touch of the divine, and they do more to fill out life and make it lovely than all our other treasures and possessions. Thank God we are not made simply of muscle, bone, nerve, and brain, and gold and possessions, but of memories, affections, associations, and soul and passions, and thoughts sweeter than kisses, and poetry without words, and music that cannot be uttered. We are made up of such things as Hadad felt when he answered, "I cannot explain it, but please allow me to go anyway."

LIFE LESSON

Sentiments for home and family and nation run deep in our lives because God has formed them in us. Never dismiss their tug on your heart as though they were foolish sentimentality or a waste of time or unspiritual nonsense. Give them their proper place in your life. Cherish them. Guard them. Let them be your treasure. Always be faithful to what God has bonded you to in life.

J. G. GREENHOUGH

HANNAH

The Nobody Who Gave Up Her Heart's Treasure

There was a certain man from Ramathaim, a Zuphite from the hill country of Ephraim, whose name was Elkanah. . . . He had two wives; one was called Hannah and the other Peninnah. Peninnah had children, but Hannah had none.

Year after year this man went up from his town to worship and sacrifice to the LORD Almighty at Shiloh, where Hophni and Phinehas, the two sons of Eli, were priests of the LORD. Whenever the day came for Elkanah to sacrifice, he would give portions of the meat to his wife Peninnah and to all her sons and daughters. But to Hannah he gave a double portion because he loved her, and the LORD had closed her womb. And because the LORD had closed her womb, her rival kept provoking her in order to irritate her. This went on year after year. Whenever Hannah went up to the house of the LORD, her rival provoked her till she wept and would not eat. Elkanah her husband would say to her, "Hannah, why are you weeping? Why don't you eat? Why are you downhearted? Don't I mean more to you than ten sons?"

1 SAMUEL 1:1-8

. . . . ● ● ● ● ● . . . .

H ANNAH WAS AN OBSCURE WIFE of an obscure man who lived in the obscure hill country of Ephraim, and yet her life has become an example of persevering prayer and deep commitment to God. She was married to Elkanah, an obvious man of worship, who appeared to be strong in his faith and attentively took his entire family to Shiloh to offer sacrifices to the Lord of hosts. Theirs was a markedly religious home, yet it was shot through with one poisoning element. Elkanah's second wife, Peninnah, was a spiteful person whose cruel words were destructive to the happiness of all who lived there, especially Hannah.

Peninnah persecuted Hannah daily, laughing and mocking and jeering and provoking her to the point of tears. Her words had a mean cutting edge that took delight in reminding Hannah that the Lord had closed her womb and left her childless. To have a barren womb in the Hebrew culture was a hard burden to carry, for others often wondered what the woman had done to so displease the Lord. And as Hannah watched Peninnah bear sons and daughters to Elkanah, she probably wondered at times why she had never had the joy of holding a newborn in her arms that she might delight herself as well as her husband. Year after year this agony went on and on as Peninnah spoke her hurtful words. The worst suffering is subtle and unspeakable, and hardly to be told or to be hinted at, made up of ten thousand little things, any one of which by itself is not worthy of a moment's consideration. Just the sound of a footstep might mean an approaching sorrow or a painful memory. It is in human nature to avenge these insults, to cry out angrily against the woman with her sneering provocations. But there is something higher than human nature, something better, and something that Hannah possessed despite all she had suffered.

The years of barrenness worked deep into her soul. And as the irritating grain of sand is transformed into a precious pearl by the oyster, in the same manner Peninnah's bitter remarks worked a depth of character in Hannah's heart. She gave herself to the passion of her desire to seek the Lord until He moved on her behalf. One dominating force in her nature transfigured everything, defied difficulties, surmounted obstacles, and waited with trembling nervous patience till God came in answer to her desperate prayers.

One year, during their annual trek to Shiloh to worship, Hannah's suffering was pushed to its limit as Peninnah "provoked her till she [Hannah] wept and would not eat" (1 Samuel 1:7). So distraught was she that after the others had finished eating and drinking, Hannah began to pour out her soul to the Lord in prayer near the temple.

What is prayer if it is not the heart on fire? Prayer is not rote artic-ulations or mere words. Prayers are battles; prayers are the thun-ders of a seeking heart that call for God when He seems to be far away. We find Hannah bowed down in humility, gripped by the agony of her suffering and calling out to the Lord from the depths of her soul: "In bitterness of soul Hannah wept much and prayed to the Lord" (v. 10). She did not hold back the battles she had fought over the years in her relationship with Peninnah. She laid it all out before the Lord, bearing her soul with all its hurts.

Do we pray with that same intensity as Hannah did? When the world batters us from all sides with its blows of disappointment and loss, bitterness and remorse, inequality and unfairness, do we go before the Lord in prayer? Or do we wander around pouring out all our bitter afflictions on every listening ear, only to burden and taint their conscience. Deep down Hannah knew that only One Person could alleviate her suffering. And as Jacob wrestled with God until he found a blessing (Genesis 32:26), Hannah would not let go of God as she wrestled in prayer until her petition for a son was granted. When all is stripped away by the hardships in life, yet the soul continues to walk through the dark and blind mists of disappointment by faith alone, then all of heaven begins to move to answer that kind of faith.

Hannah's prayer on the surface seems selfish and poor in its spir-itual tone as she pleaded for a son, but the woman did not know what she was praying for altogether. Often our prayers have their origin in the divine seed placed in our hearts by God's own Spirit. God inspires the prayer, and then answers it; dictates the language, and then satis-fies the petition. Even when we do not know what to say, "the Spirit helps us in our weakness. We do not know what we ought to pray for, but the Spirit himself intercedes for us with groans that words cannot express" (Romans 8:26). So that persons who are asking for what may be called a little ordinary daily blessing may, in reality, be asking for a gift inspired by God whose influence will reach through the ages and have repercussions of the noblest kind throughout all eternity.

Hannah said, "Give me a son!" She had no idea of the destinies that was involved in that prayer. And that prayer was not her own. Her petition was but the echo of a higher voice. Herein is the mystery of prayer. There are formal and cold prayers. There are prayers that come from the lips and not the heart, and then there are prayers that are the very cry of the heart and revelations that come from God. Subdued sighings of the soul, which God prompts and regulates, and which are sent for the trial of our patience and strength so that He may give us a greater answer than our wildest imaginations ever dreamed, than our love ever dared expect!

Hannah's cry of her heart expressed a grief that could not be expressed by mere words. Her desperation was so deep that she made a vow to the Lord as she prayed by the doorpost of the Lord's temple, "O LORD Almighty, if you will only look upon your servant's misery and remember me, and not forget your servant but give her a son, then I will give him to the LORD for all the days of his life, and no razor will ever be used on his head" (v. 11). So intent was she on praying that she did not even notice who was watching her. Eli the priest was sitting on a chair by the entrance to the temple and was observing her. "Hannah was praying in her heart, and her lips were moving but her voice was not heard" (v. 12). Eli thought she was drunk and rebuked her, saying, "How long will you keep on getting drunk? Get rid of your wine" (v. 14).

People may be drunk, but not with wine! There is grief that has upon us all the effect of poison in the blood. There are anxieties that make us stagger around like drunken men. There are perplexities and adversities in this life that rip our emotions and make us look almost insane in the eyes of those who seem calm and cool on the outside. But remember that the ordinary cannot judge the extraordinary. We should be careful how we judge one another, lest we be judged. Here is Eli, a priest of the living God, calling a woman drunken—when she is passionately in worship and prayer, when she is in the depth of her distress waiting on God to answer her. There is an impassioned fervor that is not lunacy; there is a zealousness that is the sublimest serenity.

Now, Eli had been accustomed to look upon people coming to the temple to worship and see them behave themselves under certain limits. But here is something he has never seen before, and the priest of the living God, ordained and consecrated—who ought to have had a word of encouragement for the lowly woman—instantly, with that little remnant of judgment that is in the best of us, says, "You are drunk!" When will we put the better and not the worse construction on people and their actions? When will we speak hopefully to them and not with our verbal whip of condemnation! Solomon wisely admonishes us to know all the facts before we speak and pass judgment: "He who answers before listening—that is his folly and his shame" (Proverbs 18:13).

Hannah's answer to Eli's rebuke is not filled with contempt but with honesty: "I am a woman who is deeply troubled. I have not been drinking wine or beer; I was pouring out my soul to the LORD. Do not take your servant for a wicked woman; I have been praying here out of my great anguish and grief" (v. 15). Rebuked by the truth, Eli demonstrates his character as a man of God and does not answer in self-defense. Instead, realizing his mistake, he pronounces a blessing on her, "Go in peace, and may the God of Israel grant you what you have asked of him" (v. 17). And the faith in Hannah's heart grabbed on to that word, believing that her request would be granted. Not even Eli knew the petition she had made of the Lord. The text says that she rose, went and ate, and "her face was no longer downcast" (v. 18). And God remembered Hannah and gave to her a son, whom she named Samuel. As soon as he was weaned, she, with her husband, brought him to the tabernacle at Shiloh, where she had received the answer to her prayer. There she solemnly consecrated him to the service of the Lord, and Samuel became one of the great prophets of the Old Testament.

LIFE LESSON

Hannah's life is a poignant example of a woman who would not give up despite everything to the contrary. Her devotion to prayer and perseverance is a good lesson for those of us who grow weary in our particular battles of prayer. Her word to us is, "Never give up!" That is exactly what the enemy of our souls wants. When we do not see the instant answer to our prayers, do we surrender, or do we press on against all odds? Paul commands us to press on as he did: "I have fought the good fight, I have finished the race, I have kept the faith. Now there is in store for me the crown of righteousness, which the Lord, the righteous Judge, will award to me on that day—and not only to me, but also to all who have longed for his appearing" (2 Timothy 4:7-8). We have a great reward waiting for us if we do not fall back.

JOSEPH PARKER

HEMAN

The Nobody Who Saw the Depths of His Soul

All these were sons of Heman the king's seer.

1 CHRONICLES 25:5

HEMAN WAS KING DAVID'S SEER in the matters of God. Now a seer is simply a man who sees. He is just a man who has eyes in his head. Other men also have eyes, but they do not see with their eyes as a seer sees. A seer stands out among all other men in that he sees with *all* his eyes—both physical and spiritual. Heman, then, was a seer to the king.

And he was a seer in this. Heman constantly saw a sight that to most of his contemporaries was absolutely invisible. Heman saw, and saw nothing else, but his own soul. From his childhood up Heman had as good as seen nothing in the whole world but his own soul. And, after he was well on in life, he was moved by God to describe the sight of his own soul in the eighty-eighth Psalm. It is one of the darkest of all the Psalms, and well worth your read.

King David, on occasion, was a wonderful seer himself. But David had not devoted himself to the things of his own soul as Heman had. David was a man of action and enterprise, and he had many other matters to take care of besides the matters of God and of his own soul. But Heman saw nothing else. And David, discovering this gift, made Heman his seer. David sought in Heman a seer who could see sin in both David's soul and in his own when no other eye in all Israel could see it. "My sin is always before me" (Psalm 51:3), said David, when his eyes were once opened. And it was to Heman, under God, even more than to Nathan or Gad, that David owed that ever-present sight. God's first trouble with David, as with all His men, was David's sin and David's soul. And Heman had kept so close at God's school of seers that David established him as his most private, most trusted, and most highly honored seer.

"My soul is full of trouble," Heman says, speaking about himself in Psalm 88 (v. 3). We are not told what led Heman to speak and publish abroad this most despondent of Psalms. He speaks as one moved to speak by the Holy Spirit, but more than that we do not know. There is nothing in the biblical record about Heman that indicates the source of Heman's heaviness of soul and grief.

"You have put me in the lowest pit, in the darkest depths" (v. 6). Why was that? Perhaps it was to console David in one of his many inconsolable times. It might have been to show David that a saint of God who had never sinned as David had sinned, had, nevertheless, been cast by God into depths that even David had never known. Or it may have been that Heman would provide an unforgettable Psalm grievous enough for our Lord Jesus to recall it and to repeat it during His agony in the Garden of Gethsemane, which He most certainly did. Or perhaps it was because God knew that no other Psalm would so perfectly meet us at the level of our deepest need and our darkest hour. Many troubled souls have found comfort in these melancholic words of Heman.

"From my youth I have been afflicted and close to death; I have suffered your terrors and am in despair" (v. 15). Every day we hear of people being driven to despair through love, through fear, through poverty, through pain, and sometimes through religion. There were those who described the apostle Paul as out of his mind because of his great learning (Acts 26:24). Others criticized our Lord Jesus as though He was "out of his mind" (Mark 3:21). And no wonder.

To see what was in man, and what comes out of the heart of man; and to see all that with such holy eyes and with such a holy heart as Christ's, and then to understand how it all concerned Him—no mortal mind and heart could have endured the sight. It is no surprise that we hear these words from Jesus: "My soul is *overwhelmed* with sorrow to the point of death" (Mark 14:34, emphasis added). It almost drove Him to the brink of insanity. A terror at sin and a horror took possession of our Lord's soul in the garden till He was full of trouble beyond all experience and imagination of the heart of man. It was not death that troubled Him. Death is nothing. Death is nothing compared to sin. It was sin with its unquenchable fire that tore His mighty soul.

Now there was no Old Testament saint so like our Lord in all that as Heman. He suffered something in the depths of his soul that echoed in the life of Christ hundreds of years later. The same would be true of us if our eyes could see sin in a similar light.

Yet Heman takes his complaint ever further, and anything less could not be expected. It is a simple and necessary consequence of his own troubled and distracted soul. "You have taken my companions and loved ones from me; the darkness is my closest friend" (Psalm 88:18). Ask yourself, how does one live with such a disconsolate man? Friends and loved ones all have their limits. Heman had a wife and many children; he had exceptional friends, deeply spiritual friends, in David and Asaph and Jeduthan; and he literally had a whole choir full of wonderful acquaintances (1 Chronicles 25:6-8). But despite so much vibrancy surrounding his life, all that only made him feel the more alone. For the man who takes up the troubles and despairs of the soul, there is no one to share it. When our Lord took His despairing soul to His Father in the garden, the most His friends could do for Him was stay nearby and sleep.

Other saints such as David and Isaiah and Josiah and Jeremiah speak of bearing this soul agony for a period of time, but Heman carried this his entire life. As he writes this psalm, he is an old man, but there has been no relief. It has only eaten into his soul deeper and deeper. And since souls such as Heman's are absolutely bottomless and shoreless, and since the law of God is infinitely and increasingly holy and just and good, how could Heman escape being more and more troubled every day of his life. He endured it all, it appears, so that he could be more effective in his role as the seer of the king.

LIFE LESSON

· · · · · · · · · · · · · · · · · · ● ● ● ● · · · · · · · · · · · · · · · · · · ·

When God works to deepen the spiritual life of any person, He sends that person to the same school to which He sent Heman. This is always His way. "Praise be to the God and Father of our Lord Jesus Christ, the Father of compassion and the God of all comfort, who comforts us in all our troubles, so that we can comfort those in any trouble with the comfort we ourselves have received from God" (2 Corinthians 1:3-4). Our personal troubles give us the depth of soul to help others who are troubled. Who can tell what God has laid up for you to do for Him and for men's souls? He may have a second David to comfort and to transform in the generation to come—and far more. And you may be ordained to be the king's seer in the matters of God. Who can tell? Only, be ready.

ALEXANDER WHYTE

JABEZ

The Nobody Who Was a Pain to His Mother

Jabez was more honorable than his brothers. His mother had named him Jabez, saying, "I gave birth to him in pain." Jabez cried out to the God of Israel, "Oh, that you would bless me and enlarge my territory! Let your hand be with me, and keep me from harm so that I will be free from pain." And God granted his request.

1 CHRONICLES 4:9-10

THIS IS THE SIMPLE PRAYER OF JABEZ, which has recently become the theme of a best-selling book and numerous related books and ancillary products. Nothing more is actually known of this Jabez or of his brothers. That a man should be remembered for his prayer and not for what he did is a noteworthy lesson for all of us. It seems remarkable that Jabez should be introduced without description, as though he was a well-known person, and some scholars assume that he was known to those for whom the Book of Chronicles was written, either by tradition or by writings that have perished.

Jabez was distinguished in some way above his brothers. From the description of his brief but remarkably bold prayer, we might infer that he carried in his heart a deep spirituality that set him apart from others. Perhaps he was among that group of people to whom prayer almost seems natural, to study the Word of God is a delight for them, and to be deprived of these privileges is a pain for them. But while we may infer his spirituality as distinguishing his life, we must leave this mystery as insolvable and anything more than this as speculation.

We do know that his name signifies sorrow and pain, which

tells us that Jabez did not have the best of beginnings in this world. His name was a memorial to his mother's sorrow, but not a prophecy of his own. Yet Jabez appears to be animated by a concern that his life might in some way be involved with the same sorrow and pain. Nor was this an irrational conclusion. Some people are naturally born to more sorrow than others, as certainly some people are more naturally spiritual than others. We see the operation of this mystery even within the same family, where one of the children may be full of sunlight, and hope, and music, and another loaded down in the darkness of melancholy, trouble, and oppressed with countless fears. Jabez was not about to allow the pain that surrounded his birth to rule in his life and the lives of his loved ones.

Jabez is known to us as preeminently a man of prayer. The image of Jabez is graphic and beautiful. Think of the young man standing at the door of his house, looking out at the unknown and unmeasured world, listening to the conflicting voices that troubled his native air, and then turning his eyes to heaven and asking divine direction and blessing, before he would take a single step from the threshold of his home. This indeed is what every young man should do, no matter what he feels he is about to encounter.

We are told that if we acknowledge God in all our ways, He will make our paths straight (Proverbs 3:6). God was pleased by Jabez's request to come under the Lord's blessing and presence and to have his territory enlarged! God was pleased that the young man would request His presence and the strength of His hand to be with him and to keep him from harm. It is obvious from the fact that God granted these specific requests to Jabez that there was nothing of selfishness mixed in with the prayer. It is God's delight to fulfill all that is in the heart of His people when it comes to blessing the world.

With Jabez as our example, we are assured that anyone may come before the Almighty, and speak out all his heart, and receive promises of continual guidance and defense from the living God. If we could realize the certainty of this sacred communication as between earth and heaven, our whole life would be lifted to a noble level, and instead of laboring in weary prayer we should be filled with the spirit of triumphant thankfulness and praise. It lies within our power to give a whole lifetime to God.

LIFE LESSON

· · · · · · · · · · · · · · · · ● ● ● · · · · · · · · · · · · · · · ·

There is nothing that lies beyond the reach of prayer except that which lies outside the will of God. To ask God for the fullness of His blessing upon you every day of your life is to take hold of His great willingness to supply your every need and break through to a life of abundance. If you want to experience the power of prayer as Jabez did, if you want prayer to effect real change in your life, you must learn by experience to wait upon our God.

JOSEPH PARKER

JAEL, *the* WIFE *of* HEBER *the* KENITE

The Nobody Who Was Good With a Hammer

"Most blessed of women be Jael, the wife of Heber the Kenite, most blessed of tent-dwelling women. [Sisera] asked for water, and she gave him milk; in a bowl fit for nobles she brought him curdled milk. Her hand reached for the tent peg, her right hand for the workman's hammer. She struck Sisera, she crushed his head, she shattered and pierced his temple. At her feet he sank, he fell; there he lay. At her feet he sank, he fell; where he sank, there he fell—dead."

JUDGES 5:24-27

O UT OF THEIR CONTEXT, these sincere words of blessing upon Jael from the Song of Deborah read as an extreme contradiction to the unthinkable deed she performed. How does one receive a blessing for what appears to be a cold-hearted killing, driving a tent spike into some guy's head with her own hands? What could possibly justify such raw barbarity, we are inclined to ask today? Before we enter into judgment, some background for the motive of what she did must be considered.

Similar to Rahab and Ruth, Jael was not Jewish by birth. She was a stranger to the commonwealth of Israel, one who was drawn by a spiritual affinity to the people of Yahweh and showed by her actions the reality and power of her faith. The Kenites were the family from which Moses had taken his wife (Judges 1:16), and it is thought the Kenites were a Midianite tribe (Numbers 10:29). They showed kindness to Israel in their journey through the wilderness and had their place in the settlement of the Promised

Land. But their allotment was in the south of Israel, while Heber and Jael are here found in the extreme north, pitching their tents near Harosheth. Heber had entered into friendly relations with Jabin, a king of Canaan, specifically king of Hazor (Judges 4:11, 17), and an obvious enemy of Israel. One would have assumed that this Bible nobody shared her husband's sentiments, but Sisera, Jabin's military commander, would find out to the contrary.

The power of Jabin was supreme in the northern land of Lebanon, and Sisera was stationed in the southern regions of his dominion and was in command of a vast host of nine hundred iron chariots, with which he invaded northern Israel for twenty years. The Israelites were helpless to stop his cruel oppression. Anarchy and terror stalked through the country hand in hand. The trade caravans between Tyre and the Jordan Valley, which were the means of civilizing the district, ceased. Even travelers stayed away from the highways, tormented as they were by the ruthless and predatory invader.

Jael had watched from the tents of Heber as year after year Sisera and his chariots swept past to make their accustomed raid on northern Israel. She had seen the plunderers return, leading captives, "a girl or two for each man," as well as highly embroidered garments and other domestic goods (Judges 5:30). A woman who has a woman's heart will shudder at the sight of other women, let alone girls, in the clutches of brutish conquerors. It is possible that she even knew some of those girls and their families. It is certain that she knew the fate of these poor innocents.

A filthy bandit such as Sisera, warring against a defenseless people with unrestrained license and lust for twenty years, becomes abhorrent and hateful. And apart from all these natural sentiments of womanhood, Jael was, as the Song of Deborah (Judges 5) implies, herself an Israelite in heart. To her Yahweh was God, and the promoters of cruelty and vice that were worshiped as gods by the Canaanites filled her with a secret loathing that burned within her. Sisera was the Osama bin Laden of Jael's day.

To Jael's surprise and apparent delight, the tables were finally turned on Sisera when his army was utterly defeated by the army of Deborah and Barak (Judges 4:12-22). Now Sisera, the bloodthirsty ravisher of human flesh, ran like a chicken from the conflict and pled with Jael for refuge in her tent. Had Jael aided in the escape of Sisera, as he expected she would, he would have been quick to rouse the passions of the Canaanites and returned in a raid of retaliation far more terrible than any he had previously delivered. While Sisera lived, there would have been no real deliverance for Israel.

Jael saw at once the vulnerability of the terrorist as well as her opportunity to rid the earth of a human devil. Despite the fact that her husband was in league with Sisera's king, she did not hesitate to act. In an act of almost unparalleled heroism, with a tent pin in one hand and a workman's hammer in the other, she battered in his head and pierced the man's skull.

Many have taken exception to the assassination under any circumstances. Some deny the right of any person to take the life of another, no matter how criminal or monstrous or deviant that person may be. But criticism of this sort is unhistorical as is seen in the hero status Jael was given. The important feature of the achievement is its leonine courage. The courage is derived from a faith in God and a zealous wrath against heinous sin. The Canaanite captain, whom even Barak had feared, and from whom all foes had fled for twenty years, found his match in a woman who had no military training or weapons to use in her own defense.

But because she rose to the great occasion and single-handedly was the executioner of the vengeance of God, Israel was saved and the land enjoyed peace and rest for forty years (Judges 5:31). Girls within Israel could live without the daily fear of suddenly being stolen away from their families and ravaged in a foreign land. Life could go on. Blessings to Jael!

LIFE LESSON

There comes a time for taking bold action against sin in whatever form it has invaded our lives. It might involve taking a moral stand on an issue at work, or breaking off a relationship that we know is not right, or finally saying no to a temptation we have yielded to countless times, and it may involve a risk. But true faith in God is courageous and will not surrender to a life of sin. True faith brings deliverance and freedom in the name of Jesus Christ.

JOSEPH PARKER

JETHRO

The Nobody Who Knew How to Meddle the Right Way

The next day Moses took his seat to serve as judge
for the people, and they stood around him from morning till evening.
When his father-in-law saw all that Moses was doing for the people,
he said, "What is this you are doing for the people?
Why do you alone sit as judge, while all these people
stand around you from morning till evening?"

Moses answered him, "Because the people come to me to seek God's
will. Whenever they have a dispute, it is brought to me, and I decide
between the parties and inform them of God's decrees and laws."

Moses' father-in-law replied, "What you are doing is not good. You
and these people who come to you will only wear yourselves out.
The work is too heavy for you; you cannot handle it alone."

EXODUS 18:13-18

. . . . ● ● ● ● . . . .

THE WORK THAT MOSES WAS ATTEMPTING to do in his own strength gives us a clear picture of the strong character of the man. Years before, when he lived in Pharaoh's court, he undertook to settle a dispute between an Egyptian and a Hebrew in his own strength, and he ended up killing the Egyptian (Exodus 2:11-12). When he saw two Hebrews fighting with each other, he also tried to interpose and solve their problems through his own strength (Exodus 2:13-14). And when he fled Egypt and came upon the shepherds ill-treating the daughters of Jethro, he took action by himself and delivered the maidens from their oppressors (Exodus 2:17). It would take forty long years of training on the back side of the desert for Moses to learn that true strength comes from God alone.

Yet in the text before us, we see precisely some of the same characteristics of self-reliance that Moses had demonstrated in his younger years. There is no question that he had learned to depend on God for strength. Otherwise, he never would have been able to face Pharaoh and announce God's judgments on Egypt for not releasing the people of Israel. Now, however, he was the sovereign of Israel, and he had a tremendous weight of responsibility on his shoulders of leading all these people to the Promised Land. And as leader, he administered all matters, great and small. It was a daunting task!

You have to realize that there were probably about a million Israelites at the time of the Exodus. That's a lot of people to govern for one man, especially if they all knew they could get a personal appointment with Moses to solve their differences. Think of the logistics of all those people waiting in line to present their case before Moses. He spent all his time trying to settle disputes and inform the people of God's decrees and laws. Without realizing it, Moses was fast approaching a head-on crash with burnout. He was so taken up with what had developed as a "normal" routine that he didn't foresee what was coming down the pike. His "normal" routine meant sitting all day long, from dawn to dusk, deciding every minor argument that came up in the camp.

Now at that time Jethro, Moses' father-in-law, had heard of all that God had done for Moses, and how He had brought the people of Israel up out of Egypt (Exodus 18:1). Moses had earlier sent his wife, Zipporah, and two sons, Gershom and Eliezer, back to her land. Jethro sent word to Moses that he was coming out to see him and was bringing Moses' family with him: "I, your father-in-law Jethro, am coming to you with your wife and her two sons" (Exodus 18:6).

Moses goes out to meet his father-in-law and bows down and kisses him in a greeting of respect. Hospitality was an important custom of those lands, and it was the same gracious hospitality that Moses found in Jethro's camp when he fled Egypt so many years ago. Now Moses extends the same hospitality when he invites Jethro to his tent. As Moses begins to tell his father-in-law all that God had done to Pharaoh and the Egyptians for Israel's sake, we get some insight into the kind of man Jethro was. Moses undoubtedly had introduced Jethro to the true God, and Jethro's wholehearted response to God is seen in his reply to all that Moses tells him: "Jethro was delighted to hear about all the good things the LORD had done for Israel in rescuing them from the hand of the Egyptians. He said, 'Praise be to the LORD, who rescued you from the hand of the Egyptians and of Pharaoh . . . Now I know that the LORD is greater than all other gods," (Exodus 18:9-11). He further demonstrates his faith in God by offering a burnt offering and other sacrifices to God (v. 12).

During his visit with Moses, one day Jethro comes and observed Moses as he sits and judges all the cases that are brought before him. Picture Jethro standing off to the side watching as countless Israelites come before Moses' tent hour after hour and present every imaginable dispute possible to be decided on. After a while, he approaches Moses and asks a simple question: "What is this you are doing for the people?" (Exodus 18:14) It took the common-sense wisdom of an older man than Moses to see the consequences of all that exhausting work that went on uninterrupted every day. Though Jethro may have been a simple herder, he had a keen insight into the ways of men. Though some may question what a desert nobody might have to offer to a man who had been trained in the best universities of Egypt, Jethro's profound wisdom helps lift a great burden from Moses' overwhelming responsibilities.

It's safe to assume that at first Moses was caught up by the excitement of the situation. The Israelites had just left Egypt after being enslaved for 400 years. The Exodus was an impressive display of God's power over the entire nation of Egypt. The ten plagues were so overwhelming in their effect that word of the God of Israel had spread all the way to the nations that lived in Canaan, causing them to fear (Joshua 2:8-10).

Moses was committed to his role as leader and loved his work, but Jethro, his father-in-law, had the insight to see that an increase of this kind of demanding work would soon wear out the strongest and boldest man in all the tribes of Israel. The worker in the midst of the battle is not in a position to judge so completely and certainly as the wise man who observes the scene from a distance.

Out of love for our friends and family, we should do exactly what Jethro did for his son-in-law. It may not be easy in some cases, but at times we need to speak up and point out to a friend or loved one when they are working too much and wasting all their energies that might be beneficently exercised through a longer period of time. Some people live intensely. They do not pause, nor do they take any day off as a Sabbath rest. With an unwise extravagance they expend all their energies within a brief hour.

It was upon this principle that Jethro proceeded when he asked Moses, "Why do you alone sit as judge, while all these people stand around you from morning till evening?" (v. 14) Moses, the great leader of Israel, though leading a life of arduous self-sacrifice, was actually falling below the requirements of social justice. He seemed to be acting on the conviction that only he could manage, arrange, and otherwise successfully administer all the affairs of the people. It never occurred to him that he was allowing the talents of others to lie idle.

Talent not put to use will soon wither and die if it is not encouraged. It needs to be called forth and nurtured by experience and mentoring. That's hard to do if someone is dominating the scene all the time. It is true indeed that genius asserts itself and clears for itself space and prominence equal to its measure of supremacy. On the other hand, it is equally true that an abundance of sound ability may become dormant, simply because the leaders of society do not call it into responsible exercise. The counsel that Moses received from Jethro inspired Israel with new life. From the moment Moses acted upon it, the latent talent among all of Israel rose to the occasion. Men who had probably been sulking in the background came to be recognized and honored as wise statesmen and cordial allies to help govern all the tribes of Israel. Recognizing the gifts and abilities of others and using them in a meaningful way often breaks down the walls of contention and brings about a greater unity.

Yet even in his counsel, Jethro still was wise enough to honor the place of authority God had given Moses. Moses' position was still supreme and undisputed. With honest men appointed to judge the simple cases, Moses' tremendous load as leader was lightened overnight. If Moses had continued with the status quo, who knows what would have happened. At the right moment, a word of wisdom came from someone Moses already had a respected relationship with. Sometimes we are so caught up in the thick of life with all its challenges and problems that we can't see the forest through the trees. We need to be open to those choice words of wisdom that may come from a friend or family member.

We get a glimpse into Jethro's character by the wise and prudent advice he gives Moses. Listen to his words: "But select capable men from all the people—men who fear God, trustworthy men who hate dishonest gain—and appoint them as officials over thousands, hundreds, fifties and tens. Have them serve as judges for the people at all times, but have them bring every difficult case to you; the simple cases they can decide themselves. That will make your load lighter, because they will share it with you. If you do this and God so commands, you will be able to stand the strain, and all these people will go home satisfied" (Exodus 18:21-23).

First of all, Jethro avoided the common cause of strife in decisions for leadership positions: partiality. He told Moses to pick capable men from the whole camp, which would provide an equal representation among all the tribes. Next, he stressed the importance of honest and upright men who would judge with fairness and not turn their head with a bribe for dishonest gain. The advice to appoint leaders over specific numbers would help to avoid the very problem that was wearing Moses out. By appointing leaders over numbers of 1,000, 100, 50, and 10, a more efficient and expedient system was established in the camp to solve cases, which no doubt saved an immense amount of time. But the greatest advice of all is seen in Jethro's humility when he said that everything he had suggested needed to be submitted to what God would decide: "If you do this and God so commands . . ." (v. 23). The advice Jethro gave did not cut Moses off totally from sitting as judge. Every difficult case that was beyond those who had been appointed was to be referred to Moses' well-tried judgment. In all cases of contention, his voice was to determine the counsels of the camp. In other words, his word was final!

Sometimes the relinquishing of major responsibilities leaves a vacuum in people's lives, but Jethro was wise to direct Moses at what he was best at doing. He told Moses that he needed to spend his time focusing on interceding for the people and teaching them God's laws and decrees so that they could pass them on to their children and prepare them for entering the Promised Land (vv. 19-20). The highest of all vocations is the spiritual calling. It is greater to pray than to rule. Moses was to set himself at the highest end of individual, political, and religious life of Israel, and to occupy the position of intercessor. He was to be the living link between the people and their God. Jethro's timely advice had a profound effect on the entire nation of Israel. And the fact that it was heeded by Moses, who most assuredly would have consulted with God, proves that it was God's will as well. Because Moses listened to Jethro's advice and heeded it, his life took on a higher calling of intercessor, which proved even more beneficial for the people he was leading.

LIFE LESSON

· · · · · · · · · · · · · · · ● ● ● ● ● · · · · · · · · · · · · · · ·

Have you come to a crossroad in life where you do not know what to do? Be open to hear God's answer for whatever you are facing. Because God knows our life, His answers often come from those we already love and respect, and who know us well. The question may not be whether you are doing enough for God, but whether you are doing too much in a particular direction that is wearing you out. God has His Jethros available and ready with that choice word of wisdom for the difficult situation you may be facing. Or you might be called to be like Jethro, always seeking the Lord, ready to have the right word for the occasion: "A word aptly spoken is like apples of gold in settings of silver" (Proverbs 25:11).

JOSEPH PARKER

JOSEPH *of* ARIMATHEA

The Nobody Who Finally Came Out of Hiding

Joseph of Arimathea, a prominent member of the Council,
who was himself waiting for the kingdom of God, went boldly
to Pilate and asked for Jesus' body. Pilate was surprised to hear
that he was already dead. Summoning the centurion, he asked him
if Jesus had already died. When he learned from the centurion
that it was so, he gave the body to Joseph. So Joseph bought
some linen cloth, took down the body, wrapped it in the linen,
and placed it in a tomb cut out of rock. Then he rolled a stone
against the entrance of the tomb.

MARK 15:43-46

. . . . ● ● ● ● . . . .

I T WAS A VERY DARK DAY for the Church of God that day on Golgotha when the Lord Jesus died. The sun of their souls had been eclipsed by the dark night of death. And all the disciples had forsaken Him in those final hours. The very sad words of Jesus had come true, "But a time is coming, and has come, when you will be scattered, each to his own home. You will leave me all alone. Yet I am not alone, for my Father is with me" (John 16:32). Jesus was dead upon the cross, and His enemies rejoiced that this was the end of Him.

A few women who had remained about the foot of the cross, true to the very last, were found faithful unto death, but what could they do to obtain His sacred body and give it an honorable burial? His body seemed to be in danger of the fate that usually awaited the bodies of common criminals. The fear was that it might be hurled into the first grave that could be found to shelter it.

At that perilous moment Joseph of Arimathea, of whom we've never heard of before, and of whom we never hear again, suddenly made his appearance. He was the very man needed for the occasion, a man of influence, a man possessing that kind of influence that was most effective with Pilate—a rich man, a counselor, a member of the Sanhedrin, a person of significance and character. Joseph of Arimathea certainly was known in the religious society of the day, but for certain personal reasons, personal fears, he chose to remain a nobody regarding his faith in Jesus. But the death of Jesus broke down his fear of what others thought, and he stepped forward to render an honorable service.

Every one of the four Gospels mentions Joseph of Arimathea and tells us something about him. And from them we learn that he was a disciple "who was himself waiting for the kingdom of God" (Mark 15:43). Joseph had not been so open about his following after the Lord, but now he came boldly before Pilate and asked for the body of Jesus, and without hesitation Pilate gave it to him.

Let this be remembered for your encouragement in the cloudy and dark day. If you live in any place where the faithful fail from among men, do not wring your hands in grief and sit down in despair, as though it is all over with the cause you love. The Lord lives, and He will yet keep a faithful remnant alive on this earth. Another Joseph of Arimathea will come forward at the desperate moment. Just when we cannot do without him the man will be found. There was a Joseph for Israel in Egypt, and there was a Joseph for Jesus on the cross. A Joseph acted to Him a father's part at His birth, and another Joseph arranged for His burial. The Lord will not be left without friends during those crucial times.

Joseph of Arimathea serves as *a warning for us*. He was a disciple of Christ, but the Bible says he followed Jesus secretly "because he feared the Jews" (John 19:38). John's Gospel adds that

Nicodemus, a secret disciple of the night, helped Joseph to wrap Jesus' body with spices in strips of linen for burial in accordance with Jewish burial customs (John 19:39-40). Fear that leads us to conceal our faith is an evil thing. Be a disciple by all means, but not secretly. You miss a great part of your life's purpose if you are. Above all, do not be a disciple secretly because of the fear of man, for the fear of man is a hindrance to faith. Be careful to give honor to Christ openly, and He will take care of your honor.

What possibly intimidated Joseph of Arimathea from being an open follower of Jesus was the fact that he was *a rich man*. A sad truth lies within our Lord's exclamation, "It is hard for a rich man to enter the kingdom of heaven" (Matthew 19:23). Although wealth is a great resource that may be well used by the man or woman who has entered into the kingdom of heaven, it does bring with it plenty of temptations. And when a person has not yet entered into the kingdom, in many ways it is a terrible hindrance to that person's entrance.

It goes without doubt that Joseph of Arimathea missed out on many blessings by his secrecy, for he did not live with Jesus, as many other disciples did. During that brief but golden period in which men walked and talked, and ate and drank with Jesus, Joseph was not with Him learning the truths of the kingdom of God. He lost out on many of those familiar talks with which the Lord indulged His own after the multitudes had been sent away. Joseph missed that sacred training and strengthening that equipped men for the noble lives of those first saints.

Joseph of Arimathea is not just a warning; he is also a lesson for *our instruction*. Joseph finally did come out into the open with others about his faith. But what was it that drew him out? *It was the undeniable power of the cross!* Is it not remarkable that all the life of Christ did not draw out an open confession from this man? Jesus' miracles, His marvelous teachings, His poverty and self-renunciation, His glorious life of holiness and benevolence, all may have helped to build up Joseph in his secret faith, but it did not suffice to develop in him a bold confession of faith to those around him. The shameful death of the cross had greater power over Joseph than all the beauty of Christ's life.

If you are honest and sincere about your faith, sooner or later you will have to openly confess your Lord. Do you not think it would be better to make it sooner rather than later? I suppose that to Joseph of Arimathea Christ's death on the cross seemed such a *wicked thing* that he must come out on behalf of one treated so evilly. If you are a secret disciple, will you not step out of your hiding place? When you hear His deity denied, when His headship in the Church is given to another, when you hear the name of Jesus blasphemed, as it is in these evil days, will you not stand up for Him? His cause is that of truth and righteousness, and mercy and hope for all the sons of men; therefore, He must not be abused while you sit by in silence.

Do you not think Joseph stood there and listened to all the obscenities and scorn heaped upon the dying Lord? Since Jesus would not speak for Himself, but remained dumb as a sheep before its shearers, Joseph felt compelled to open his mouth for Him. The wonders of Jesus' death had convinced even the centurion that this was a righteous man. How much more Joseph, who knew more of Jesus and all that He had taught? The time came when he would need to act boldly as Christ's disciple. In going to Pilate to request Jesus' body, he put himself under personal risk. He also brought upon himself ceremonial pollution in touching a dead body, especially during the Passover week. Joseph handled that blessed body and defiled himself in the judgment of his fellow Jews. But for him, it was neither of these. For Joseph, it was an honor. Dishonor for Christ is honor, and shame for Him is the very top of all glory.

LIFE LESSON

Do not stand in the shadows of fear as Joseph of Arimathea did for so long. Dare to come out and be numbered with those who believe and follow Jesus Christ. Every man or woman who loves Jesus Christ proves it by his or her actions at those crucial times. For the Word of God says, "Whoever acknowledges me before men, I will also acknowledge him before my Father in heaven. But whoever disowns me before men, I will disown him before my Father in heaven" (Matthew 10:32-33).

CHARLES SPURGEON

JOSHEB-BASSHEBETH, ELEAZAR, and SHAMMAH

The Nobodies Who Risked Their Lives for a Drink of Water

These are the names of David's mighty men: Josheb-Basshebeth, a Tahkemonite, was chief of the Three; he raised his spear against eight hundred men, whom he killed in one encounter.

Next to him was Eleazar son of Dodai the Ahohite. As one of the three mighty men, he was with David when they taunted the Philistines gathered at Pas Dammim for battle. Then the men of Israel retreated, but he stood his ground and struck down the Philistines till his hand grew tired and froze to the sword. The LORD brought about a great victory that day. The troops returned to Eleazar, but only to strip the dead.

Next to him was Shammah son of Agee the Hararite. When the Philistines banded together at a place where there was a field full of lentils, Israel's troops fled from them. But Shammah took his stand in the middle of the field. He defended it and struck the Philistines down, and the LORD brought about a great victory.

2 SAMUEL 23:8-13

· ● ● ● ● ·

D AVID WAS THIRTY YEARS OLD when he became king of Israel, and he reigned for forty years (2 Samuel 5:4). During his reign, he was surrounded by a group of mighty men who served him with unflinching loyalty, but of that group, three are mentioned as outstanding warriors above all the rest. They were famous in the highest degree for their devotion to David as a person and his cause. The names of those three were:

Josheb-Basshebeth, a Tahkemonite; Eleazar the son of Dodo the Ahohite; and Shammah the son of Agee the Hararite. Instead of remaining nameless nobodies in the ranks of the common soldiers, these men excelled beyond all others and become "warrior" somebodies, forever remembered as David's Mighty Men. What an honor!

Can a finer picture of devotion be found than is seen in the admirable loyalty these three men gave to David? To pledge themselves to serve David with their very lives speaks of their character and their commitment to David as their king. Israel knew that it was God who had appointed Saul as their first king. And when Saul walked in disobedience and displeased God, the Lord sent his prophet Samuel to rebuke Saul and then anoint David as Saul's successor. Those three men would have known without a doubt that Samuel had anointed David as the next king of Israel, according to the Lord's command: "So Samuel took the horn of oil and anointed him in the presence of his brothers, and from that day on the Spirit of the LORD came upon David in power" (1 Samuel 16:13).

Knowing that the Spirit of the Lord had come upon David that day solidified in their consciences a resolute determination and an indomitable spirit to serve him no matter what the cost. They knew beyond a shadow of doubt that David was divinely selected to lead the nation. That surety of purpose became their bulwark of strength every time they went into battle and faced staggering odds. Having the assurance that God was behind their king caused them to display amazing courage, and an insightful phrase occurs a number of times in the battle accounts of these three mighty men: ". . . and the LORD brought about a great victory" (2 Samuel 23:10, 12). Their superb military training and their distinguished bravery gained them victories, which according to the text were referred to as the Lord's victories against David's enemies.

In one battle against the Philistines, Eleazar is said to have "stood his ground and struck down the Philistines till his hand grew tired and froze to the sword" (v. 10). There are well-authenticated instances of severe cramps following excessive exertion, so much so that the soldier's hand could only be released from the sword by external force.

To appreciate the victory won by Shammah (2 Samuel 23:11-12), we need to understand some of the history of Israel's relationship to the Philistines. The Israelites had suffered greatly at the hands of the Philistines for years during the period of the judges. They lived in constant dread of being attacked, even to the point that they refused to use their main roads and traveled on winding paths (Judges 5:6).The Philistines had even removed every weapon from among the Israelites and made sure that no blacksmith lived in the land to prevent them from making weapons to defend themselves (1 Samuel 13:19). They had pillaged their villages and carried off their livestock and crops. When the Philistines gathered at a field full of lentils they probably were going to raid, Shammah stood his ground when the rest of Israel's troops fled. We read, "But Shammah took his stand in the middle of the field. He defended it and struck the Philistines down, and the LORD brought about a great victory" (v. 12).

On one occasion, David was in his stronghold, the cave of Adullam, and in distress said, "Oh, that someone would get me a drink of water from the well near the gate of Bethlehem!" (v. 15) He was reminiscing of the times when he could drink from that well. There are times when memory goes back to the earliest scenes of life, when only old faiths, old habits, old pastors, old friends, can really minister to the hunger and thirst in our lives. An old man is said to live more in his early years than in the times that are passing around him. What is true in general life is significantly and profoundly true in spiritual experiences. We become dissatisfied with the new, the modern, the last invention, and go back to old times, that we may rest in the house of our youth, and pray at the altar that we built at the first.

Any good water would have quenched David's thirst, but in the moment of his agony, he longed for water from the well of Bethlehem. What follows in the text is a demonstration of why these three mighty men were worthy of their fame. They were not merely ornamental personages in the army or in the court. Looking at them in what in our own day we would call their honors, their badges, their medals, or their other decorations, one might wonder how they came to be so set apart from the others who fought for David. Our wonder is more than satisfied by the deeds they accomplished out of their loyalty to their king: "So the three mighty men broke through the Philistine lines, drew water from the well near the gate of Bethlehem and carried it back to David. But he refused to drink it; instead, he poured it out before the LORD" (v. 16).

They were men of daring, men of the highest valor, men whose spirit was subdued and ennobled by supreme loyalty and consecration to David. We would do well to apply the same test to our own standing and quality as those who profess to follow Christ as our King. As our leader, the firstborn from the dead, our Lord is continually expressing desires. What are we doing to prove that we are willing to make them a reality in our world as we enter the twenty-first century? He desires that His Word be spread abroad to the ends of the earth (Matthew 28:19-20). He desires that His Church shine as a pure bride, the fairest among all the objects seen by men (Ephesians 5:25-27; Revelation 21:9). Who is valiant enough to stand up in this hour to defy the enemy, to drive away the devastator, and to protect His Church from incursions of this world's corrupt value system (1 John 2:15-17)? Christ desires that the poor be fed and clothed (Matthew 25:35-40). He wants the ignorant taught, the oppressed delivered, the heart-broken comforted (Isaiah 61:1-3).

Who has strength enough of mind and pureness enough of consecration to abandon all the charms of earthly vanity and glory, and give himself wholly to the cause of humanity as represented in the

Son of Man? There is a fame not worth having—a fame of mere words, a noise of popularity, a fickle wind that follows men only so long as they are content to be driven by it. Let our fame be established upon our willingness to serve our King in whatever He commands, for then we will inherit the imperishable crown of life (James 1:12).

LIFE LESSON

David's mighty men were limited to a few out of all those who fought in his army, but God desires that all who come to Him through faith in His Son become mighty in the work of extending His kingdom here on earth. But the narrow path to that greatness goes against the world's idea of attaining fame. Jesus said, "For even the Son of Man did not come to be served, but to serve, and to give his life as a ransom for many" (Mark 10:45). Being mighty in God's eyes is one who does not exalt himself but rather humbles himself and gives himself in love to serve others. Each of us has a gifting that God has given us by His Spirit, and it is our duty to return it to Him by using it to serve others to bring them to the knowledge of our Lord Jesus Christ. We must allow Him to make us a "vessel unto honour, sanctified, and meet for the master's use, and prepared unto every good work" (2 Timothy 2:21, KJV).

JOSEPH PARKER

JUBAL

The Nobody Who Made People Dance

*His brother's name was Jubal; he was the father
of all who play the harp and flute.*

GENESIS 4:21

· ● ● ● ● ● ● ·

THE BIBLE HAS A WAY OF ITS OWN of setting the distinctness in families. Over and above, and sometimes entirely superseding the original and natural order of father and son, the Bible sets up an intellectual, a moral, and a spiritual order of fatherhood and sonship. Such is the case with Jubal, an obscure nobody tucked away in a short genealogical list. While the Bible is silent as to naming any of his natural children, we are told that he became the father of all who play the harp and flute.

Early in mankind's story, Jubal took to inventing and perfecting his harp and flute. Perhaps the melodious soul of Jubal was so pained by the sin he saw in the pre-flood world around him that he rose up and said, "If the men and women of my generation are going to rebel and forget God, I will make melody to God with a string instrument and with a praise-breathing flute. As for me and my house, we shall make melody in our hearts to God." And so he did. And Jubal lived and added string after string to his harp and hollowed out one flute after another until God's angels came and took Jubal home to his harp of gold.

By the time of Moses and Aaron, Jubal had a whole tribe to himself of sons and daughters in those melodious men and women who rose up and called him their true father and blessed his honored name (Exodus 15:1). Do you suppose that Jubal's great name was ungratefully forgotten on the shore of the Red Sea that morning?

153

Do you think it as they sang out these words: "Who among the gods is like you, O LORD? Who is like you—majestic in holiness, awesome in glory, working wonders?" (Exodus 15:11) Then Miriam, the prophetess, the sister of Aaron, took a tambourine in her hand, and all the women went after her with tambourines and dancing (Exodus 15:20). These are the sons and daughters of Jubal.

And after the schools of the prophets arose in Israel, Jubal's name would be written in letters of gold upon the lintels and the doorposts of those ancient homes of religion and learning and art. When Samuel anointed Saul as king of Israel, he said, "As you approach the town, you will meet a procession of prophets coming down from the high place with lyres, tambourines, flutes and harps being played before them, and they will be prophesying. The Spirit of the LORD will come upon you in power, and you will prophesy with them; and you will be changed into a different person" (1 Samuel 10:5-6). Jubal would be pleased with his heritage among the prophets.

Then came the worship in the temple of Solomon, the house of the Lord at Jerusalem. If you would see a great host of Jubal's children at their highest honors, come up to Jerusalem at one of the great feasts. Note the emphasis that King David gave to the worship of God. When he was old and made Solomon king, he committed 24,000 Levites to the work of the temple, 6,000 to be officials and judges, 4,000 to be gatekeepers, and *4,000 to praise the Lord with musical instruments he had provided for that purpose* (1 Chronicles 23:1-5). And again, "He stationed the Levites in the temple of the LORD with cymbals, harps and lyres in the way prescribed by David and Gad the king's seer and Nathan the prophet; this was commanded by the LORD through his prophets. So the Levites stood ready with David's instruments, and the priests with their trumpets. . . . When the offerings were finished, the king and everyone present with him knelt down and worshiped. King Hezekiah and his officials ordered the Levites to praise the LORD with the words of David and of Asaph the seer. So they sang praises with gladness and bowed their heads and worshiped" (2 Chronicles 29:25-30). The temple in Jerusalem was the earthly palace of Israel's heavenly King; and for riches, for beauty, and for melody of voices and instruments of music, God gave commandment that His earthly temple should be made as near to the pattern of His heavenly temple as the hands of His people could make it.

There is in music and in song a mysterious and a mighty power to stir the heart with high and grand emotions. Music has the amazing ability to raise the heart above time and feelings to the love and pursuit of heavenly things. The great Reformer, Martin Luther, said, "The fairest and most glorious gift of God is music. Kings and princes and great lords should give their support to music. Music is a discipline; it is an instructress; it makes people milder and gentler, more moral, and more reasonable." "Music," he says in another place, "is a fair and glorious gift of God, and takes its place next to theology. It has often given me new life and inspired me with a desire to preach."

And it began with one man, Jubal, the father of all who play the harp and the flute.

LIFE LESSON

Since the days of Jubal, nothing has changed regarding our relationship to worshiping the Lord. "Praise the LORD, all you servants of the LORD who minister by night in the house of LORD. Lift up your hands in the sanctuary and praise the LORD. May the LORD, the Maker of heaven and earth, bless you from Zion" (Psalm 134). Come with a broken and contrite spirit and bring a psalm, a hymn, or a spiritual song with a harp or with a flute or with what you will. But come and worship the Lord.

ALEXANDER WHYTE

THE LITTLE BOY
and the FEEDING *of the*
FIVE THOUSAND

The Nobody Whose 50¢ Lunch Went a Long Way

*When Jesus looked up and saw a great crowd coming toward him,
he said to Philip, "Where shall we buy bread for these people to eat?"
He asked this only to test him, for he already had in mind
what he was going to do.*

*Philip answered him, "Eight months' wages would not
buy enough bread for each one to have a bite!"*

*Another of his disciples, Andrew, Simon Peter's brother, spoke up,
"Here is a boy with five small barley loaves and two small fish,
but how far will they go among so many?"*

JOHN 6:5-10

· · · · · · · · · · · · · · · · · · ● ● ● ● ● · · · · · · · · · · · · · · · · · · ·

J ust a boy in a vast sea of faces. We don't even know his name or who his parents were. Was he a little peddler who, seeing the big crowd, thought he could make a fast buck or two by selling a few loaves and fish. Had he nearly sold out, and was he saving the last portion for himself? Or was he a boy whom the disciples had employed to carry this slender provision for the use of Jesus and His friends? We don't know anything about him or why he was there, but in the providence of God he was the right boy in the right place that day.

But the boy's loaves and fish were nearly despised away, for Andrew concluded, "How far will they go among so many?" Given a crowd of well over five thousand hungry people, I'm with Andrew on this one. I wonder why he even bothered to mention it. You're just wasting your breath, Andrew.

Now, I daresay that some of you have had satan whisper similar words in your heart. "What is the use of your trying to do anything for God?" To you, dear mother, with a family of children, he has lied, "You can never serve God. Look at your time commitments. Look at your skills." The devil knows very well that, by the sustaining grace of God, you can. And he is afraid of how well you can serve God if you bring up those dear children in the love of God. He says to you, "You have so little ability, and the world is so big. What can you do?" Ah, he is afraid of what you can do, and if you will only do what you can do, God will help you do what now you cannot do.

The truth is that satan is terrified of even the little that you can do now. Yet he has tricked many of God's children into siding with him in despising the day of small things. You may feel disdained even by other believers as you try to serve the Lord, so is it any wonder if you are held in contempt by the world? The things that God will honor, man will first despise. If you will run the gauntlet of the ridicule of men, you will find your place in the service of God.

Though seemingly inadequate to feed the multitude, these loaves and fish would have been quite enough for the boy's supper, yet he appears to have been more than willing to part with them at Jesus' request. The lad might easily have thought, *It's every man for himself out here. I'm just a kid, and I'm hungry. I have what I need, so I'll take care of myself first.* We do the same when we say to ourselves, "I need to make money first, and I need to get my career in place. I can always serve God later." But the boy whom God uses refuses to be selfish and is rewarded in the process. Not only is he drawn into participating directly with an amazing miracle, but he gets to eat a full meal and is allowed to share in the twelve baskets of leftovers! It was a day I'm certain he never forgot.

Can you imagine the transformation that the boy saw when his few provisions were placed in the blessed hands that one day would bear the nail prints? Is it not a wonderful thing that Christ, the living God, should associate Himself with our weaknesses, with our lack of talent, with our little faith? And yet He does so. If we are not associated with Him, we can do nothing, and the five thousand go hungry. But when we come into loving touch with Christ, we can do all things. Those few barley loaves in Christ's hands were converted into thousands that easily met the needs of the multitude. Out of His hands they are nothing but five small barley loaves, but in His hands, linked to Jesus, they are in contact with omnipotence.

The lad's meager provisions thus became the Savior's property. Jesus seemed to say to the obscure boy, "These will work just fine for Me." And then He "gave thanks" (John 6:11) for what the loaves and fish would soon accomplish. Christ gave thanks to His Father for these trinkets, but don't you think He also thanked the boy? Christ, you see, blesses our offerings, not for their worth, but because His power will yet make them worthy of His praise. The heart of Jesus is always delighted when we bring Him something of ourselves that it may be touched by His dear hand and blessed by His gracious lips.

This boy gave everything—all his loaves and all his fish, despite their insufficiency—and Christ multiplied them to relieve the misery of a tired and famished multitude. To make quite sure that we would never forget how much God can do with little things from little boys, this story is the only miracle of Jesus Christ that was recorded in all four Gospels. I cannot help but think that there is a lesson for us all here. We should never underestimate the power of God to use our lives and whatever we have to bless others.

LIFE LESSON

· ● · ● · ● ·

No matter what you feel about your abilities or life, bring all that you are and possess to Jesus so that it may be joined to Him. Bring Him your mind, which can be associated with the teachings of the Holy Spirit in the Word of God. Bring Him your heart, which can be warmed with the love of God to touch others. Bring Him your tongue, which can be touched and purified with the live coal from off the altar as Isaiah's was (Isaiah 6:5-7). In association with Christ, your abilities will be sufficient for any occasion to which God has called you. Never dwell on the inventory of your deficiencies, which you probably have updated on a daily basis. Bring what you have, and let all that you are—body, soul, and spirit—be placed in God's hands.

CHARLES SPURGEON

THE LITTLE CAPTIVE MAID

The Nobody Who Didn't Hold a Grudge

*Now Naaman was commander of the army of the king of Aram.
He was a great man in the sight of his master and highly regarded,
because through him the LORD had given victory to Aram.
He was a valiant soldier, but he had leprosy.*

*Now bands from Aram had gone out and had taken captive
a young girl from Israel, and she served Naaman's wife. She said
to her mistress, "If only my master would see the prophet who is in
Samaria! He would cure him of his leprosy." Naaman went to his
master and told him what the girl from Israel had said.*

2 KINGS 5:1-4

. . . . ● ● ● . . . .

I MAGINE FOR A MOMENT the little unknown maid of our
story who comes upon the scene of Old Testament history for
an instant and disappears forever. We are given but a brief
glimpse of a Jewish girl so fair and good who had been torn from
her home in the border skirmishes between the Aramaens and the
Israelites of Samaria. Held captive in Damascus, she found herself
in the home of Naaman, the captain of the Syrian army who had
warred against her country and carried her from her home.
Naaman was *the* enemy and a master who claimed an absolute and
tyrannical right in her small person.

She could not have been very young when she was torn from her
home, or she would not have known about Elisha, the great prophet
in Samaria. The fact that she remembered him proves that she
remembered her parents and her father's home. And, remembered,

161

these lost joys would be the poignant grief of the child's heart. Suppose that she was nine years old when she was carried away, and had reached the age of twelve when she comes for a moment upon the stage of history. During the time of her servitude that thoughtful little soul must have suffered constant anguish.

One might have expected that she would sorrow over her loss for weeks or months, but then she would accommodate herself to her new situation, adapt the sentiments and culture of her captors, and possibly even become more Syrian than the Syrians. That, however, is not the case. Despite her circumstances, she settles down to her new duties and sweetly takes up the interests around her, and never yields an inch from the constant faith in which she had been brought up. To retain the memories of the past unobliterated by sorrow and still be ready for the duties of an uncongenial present; to be surrounded by the pomp and show of idolatry and still to keep the heart set on the ways of God—she was surely a rare and noble spirit.

This fine quality of grasping one's faith with a passionate tenacity in the dark desolation of exile is one we see in many of the Jews forced into captivity. But usually it has been accompanied by an exclusiveness and a contempt for the Gentile captors. It is the tendency of human nature to balance the humiliation of misfortune by a colossal pride, and to take vengeance on those who inflict the humiliation by regarding them secretly with scorn. Now, what is so attractive in the child is that her heart remained tender and unselfish in the midst of her sufferings. No angry feeling could crush her instinctive compassion. When she saw her master decaying with that dreadful incurable disease, she was also very aware of God's saving presence with His people through His servant Elisha, and she selflessly shared that knowledge with her Aramaen captors. Despite the fact that Naaman was her enemy, she only saw that he was a captive of his living death, and that all his unquestioned valor was useless to contend against the insidious foe of leprosy.

But there was an earnestness and an impetuousness in the way she expressed her feeling that demonstrated a strong and brave nature. It required courage to speak to her mistress at all. It required still greater courage to recommend a remedy that, from its nature, implied a superiority of her native country to that of her master. She must have said it in a striking manner for it to be carried to Naaman, and even to the presence of the king. Or perhaps through a strong and holy faith she had won a place of unusual confidence in the house where she was a stranger. In any case, her counsel was taken seriously, which led the king of Syria to write the king of Israel and send the great Naaman to the court of the neighboring state in quest of a cure.

But here remains the broad and simple fact. It was the devotion and thoughtfulness, the mercy and the courage of a little unknown girl that led to an episode that is of all others in the Old Testament the most exact representation of the way by which the soul is washed from sin. The cure of the Gentile master, effected through submitting to God's method and washing in the Jordan River, proved to be but the beginning for the results. For the story of her master's cure has passed in sacred Scripture as a symbol full of redemptive meaning, and wherever the gospel is preached the deed of this child is celebrated.

LIFE LESSON

· · · · · · · · · · · · · · · · ● ● ● · · · · · · · · · · · · · · · ·

God's children, who love Him and serve Him with all their heart, often find themselves in extraordinarily difficult circumstances from which there is no divine promise of relief. We do, however, have the promise that God will always be with us and that His love in our hearts is greater than any adversity we will ever face. No matter what your age or situation in life, if you are true to your faith, you will influence those around you for God and for good.

ROBERT F. HORTON

LYDIA

The Nobody Whose Heart Was Ready

*During the night Paul had a vision of a man of Macedonia standing
and begging him, "Come over to Macedonia and help us." After Paul
had seen the vision, we got ready at once to leave for Macedonia,
concluding that God had called us to preach the gospel to them.*

*From Troas we put out to sea and sailed straight for Samothrace,
and the next day on to Neapolis. From there we traveled to Philippi,
a Roman colony and the leading city of that district of Macedonia.
And we stayed there several days.*

*On the Sabbath we went outside the city gate to the river,
where we expected to find a place of prayer. We sat down
and began to speak to the women who had gathered there.
One of those listening was a woman named Lydia, a dealer in purple
cloth from the city of Thyatira, who was a worshiper of God. The
Lord opened her heart to respond to Paul's message. When she and
the members of her household were baptized, she invited us to her
home. "If you consider me a believer in the Lord," she said,
"come and stay at my house." And she persuaded us.*

ACTS 16:9-15

． ． ． ． ． ． ． ． ． ． ． ． ． ． ． ． ． ● ● ● ● ● ． ． ． ． ． ． ． ． ． ． ． ． ． ．

ABOUT TWENTY YEARS after the death and resurrection
of Christ, there was still no Christianity in all of Europe,
except so far as a few scattered Jews, traveling for purposes of trade—or here and there a Greek sailor or Roman soldier—might have had in their hearts the seeds of Divine truth,
sown there by the words and work of Christ in Judea, or elsewhere
by some followers of Christ. It is safe to say that at this moment in
history Europe lay in spiritual darkness from one end to the other
concerning the light of the gospel.

The significance of the events that turned Paul's steps toward Europe is more clearly seen today than at the time. By divine leading, the apostle's course was blocked when he tried to go to Asia to preach the gospel. At Troas he was on the edge of Asia, with Europe on the opposite shore. There he had a vision, in which a man of Macedonia stood on the other side of the water and beckoned for aid. With the door to Asia closed, Paul took this as God's indication to carry the gospel to Europe. So Paul, Timothy, Silas, and Luke immediately started for the new mission field. Paul had learned that when God closes one door, He opens another one.

After a voyage of two days, the apostle and his companions landed at Neapolis, a Macedonian harbor, and then traveled ten miles inland to Philippi, a city built by King Philip, the father of Alexander the Great. What day the apostles landed we do not know. But since a few days elapsed before the Sabbath came round, it is clear they must have arrived early in the week. While it was useless to look around for a Christian cause, it was not unreasonable for them to try to discover a Jewish place of worship. Their practice had always been to go to their own nationality first. But there was no synagogue in Philippi.

And so Paul and his companions set off toward the river in search of a place of prayer. They found a small gathering of women, and Paul sat down and talked to them. The first gospel sermon in Europe was purely conversational. It was neither rhetorical nor anything to dazzle its listeners. It was an earnest talk for the purpose of winning a few to Christ, and not for the sake of gaining a reputation for the preacher. And the first convert in Europe happened at this simple service by the river. That convert was Lydia, an otherwise unknown nobody who had humbly come to the river to observe the Jewish Sabbath and worship.

Lydia was born at Thyatira, in the province of Asia, and probably spent most of her life there. It was business that brought her to

Philippi. Her native city was famous for its magnificent dye-works, which were sought after from all over. Purple was a favorite color with those of the ancient world. Lydia, who was "a seller of purple," may have been in Philippi selling the dye or the cloth that had passed through the coloring process.

She was a Jewish proselyte. Evidently devout by nature and habit, she was walking with God up to the full measure of her knowledge and doing her best to serve Him. Born outside the ranks of the chosen people, and without a direct share in the truths and traditions that had been passed down from Abraham and Moses and the long line of the prophets, she yet accepted the faith of Israel and was living a religious life and developing and demonstrating a religious character.

She had adopted the Hebrew faith, she worshiped God, but she was not content. Like the Ethiopian eunuch (Acts 8:26-38), she cherished longings in her heart that could scarcely be expressed in words—a hunger of love created by the very pureness of the law that she had accepted as her rule of life. She followed the ceremonies of her new religion faithfully. She observed the many washings and prayed the prayers, but inside her heart she felt an aching void. That morning by the river brought about for her a spiritual crisis and an awakening to a spiritual reality beyond all her hopes and dreams.

There are two traits worth noting with Lydia's readiness to receive the truth that Paul was speaking about. First, *she kept the Sabbath day holy.* In this heathen town of Philippi, and all over the world, the Sabbath day was unknown, except among the Jews and the proselytes of the Jewish faith. When the Sabbath day dawned, Lydia's house of business was closed. She and others gathered by the river to honor the Sabbath.

Second, *Lydia was at the place of prayer.* She was away from her native home, but she was worshiping. The faith that had come to her at Thyatira was not left behind when she traveled to Philippi. The habit of worship she had acquired in her home city was continued at Philippi. And this morning, divine providence had brought her to a place that would change her life and the history of all Europe forever.

Wherever darkness has reigned, whether in a geographical place or an individual heart, God will always try to bring the light of His truth to bear there. He placed His messenger at the right place at the right time, as he did with Paul, and began a domino effect that began to spread the message of freedom in Christ across the whole continent. Why Paul was specifically prevented from going to Asia we are not told, but the divine strategy of him crossing to Macedonia has been proven by the fruit born of that meeting by the river with Lydia.

Lydia had a nature highly sensitive to religious influences, and Paul's appeals to her spiritual hunger met with a quick response. She came under the special illumination of the Spirit of the Lord whom Paul was preaching, and her mind was quickened to understand the truth about Jesus. Her heart was made willing and even eager to receive the grace of God in Christ. The Lord opened her heart. For people like Lydia, it is not His way to use violent means, forcing open the locks of the heart. He may deal so with a rebellious spirit as He did with Saul of Tarsus—the preacher for that day. But for his gentle listener in Philippi, no such violence was necessary. Lydia went forth to meet God, trembling, and her heart was opened by consent and preparation of her will.

Lydia immediately demonstrated the sincerity and earnestness of her confession of Christ in two ways. In the first place, *she received baptism.* Not necessarily in an ostentatious manner, but in a way to make the fact known to all who had a right to know. This "seller of purple" seems to have given not so much as a passing thought to the effect that this step she was taking would have on her business. She did not ask whether it would increase or decrease her popularity. She accepted Christ, and she wanted to be baptized into the name of the Father and the Son and the Holy Spirit.

Considering all the possible repercussions, this step was a remarkable exhibition of devotion and courage.

As soon as she had entered the household of faith through baptism, Lydia *insisted on extending Christian hospitality* to those to whom she felt so greatly indebted for the new light and life they had brought to her. This was one of the first forms of service open to her, and she gave herself to it without question or hesitation. It is most likely that Lydia was a widow, and she also must have been a woman of some position, for she was able to entertain the apostle and his company.

With her they also baptized her household—either her children, or the workers in her business, and perhaps her domestic servants. It was understood that the proselyte to Judaism included his entire household. The same was sometimes done in the case of the earlier converts to Christianity. Thus the jailer of this same city of Philippi was baptized "with his household" (Acts 16:33, NASB). The whole narrative seems to indicate a feeling of solidarity in an ancient family.

When the quiet riverside scene and service came to a close, violent persecutions followed Paul and Silas. We lose sight of Lydia, but it is clear that her faithfulness was not shaken. For when Paul and Silas came out of prison, "they went to Lydia's house, where they met with the brothers and encouraged them" (Acts 16:40). Had she proved unfaithful, they would not have reentered her house and accepted her hospitality. If her love had chilled in any way, there would have been no open door for them. Thus she has become a woman of character noted by her courage and her devotion to duty. She considered opportunities of kindness toward those persecuted to be God's *reward,* not His burdens. Lydia, the first-named convert on European soil, had a tremendous effect on the little church that now gathered around her. And as it continued to grow, her influence must have remained strong, for in the house of Lydia was cradled the Philippian church—the church that the apostle Paul afterward described as his "joy and crown" (Philippians 4:1).

LIFE LESSON

L ydia's conversion is a poignant example of one whose heart was open to the stirrings of God's truth. She was not singled out for any greatness of social standing. But God does not regard position, but rather heart, and hers was wide open for the truth of Jesus Christ. It also demonstrates God's divine wisdom in dispersing the gospel to the ends of the earth. As you go forth to speak of Him, listen to the leading of His Spirit, for the next person you share the gospel with may be a key person in spreading the news of Jesus' salvation to an ever increasing number of people. "For nothing is impossible with God" (Luke 1:37).

JAMES HASTINGS

MAHLAH, NOAH, HOGLAH, MILCAH, and TIRZAH

The Nobodies Who Wanted a Piece of the Pie

The daughters of Zelophehad son of Hepher, the son of Gilead, the son of Makir, the son of Manasseh, belonged to the clans of Manasseh son of Joseph. The names of the daughters were Mahlah, Noah, Hoglah, Milcah and Tirzah. They approached the entrance to the Tent of Meeting and stood before Moses, Eleazar the priest, the leaders and the whole assembly, and said, "Our father died in the desert. He was not among Korah's followers, who banded together against the LORD, but he died for his own sin and left no sons. Why should our father's name disappear from his clan because he had no son? Give us property among our father's relatives."

So Moses brought their case before the LORD and the LORD said to him, "What Zelophehad's daughters are saying is right. You must certainly give them property as an inheritance among their father's relatives and turn their father's inheritance over to them.

Say to the Israelites, 'If a man dies and leaves no son, turn his inheritance over to his daughter. If he has no daughter, give his inheritance to his brothers. If he has no brothers, give his inheritance to his father's brothers. If his father had no brothers, give his inheritance to the nearest relative in his clan, that he may possess it. This is to be a legal requirement for the Israelites, as the LORD commanded Moses.' "

NUMBERS 27:1-8

O F ALL THE WOMEN in the camp of the Israelites, why should such names—ones even a mite difficult to pronounce—have any significant meaning? On the outside, they might seem your run-of-the-mill nobodies, but on the inside, these ladies had some pluck that was about to stir the camp of Israel and bring down any traces of machismo a peg or two.

These are the names of the five daughters of a man called Zelophehad. He was a quiet man and took no part in the great rebellion against the Lord in which Korah and his company justly perished when the ground opened up and swallowed them alive (Numbers 16:1-33). This man Zelophehad lived his appointed days and then died in his own bed. To die without having a son to pass on one's inheritance was a major issue of concern for any Israelite. According to the Law of Moses, the daughters were plumb out of luck. You see, women weren't even considered when it came to an inheritance. That was strictly male business. And now that their father was gone, these five women could not stop thinking and worrying about what was going to happen to them. The possibility of losing their father's inheritance was something that disturbed them, took away their sleep, and made them grievously discontented. After much deliberation, they determined to make a public speech and do something unheard of—challenge the laws of inheritance.

So they gathered together to encourage one another and to plan what they were going to say. This was no small undertaking they were about to venture out on, and you can be sure they were probably very nervous about what they were determined to ask for. Then they headed off toward the tabernacle to deliver the speech they had carefully prepared. And a great and intimidating audience they had—Moses, Eleazar the priest, the elders, and all the congregation of Israel—as they stood by the door of the tabernacle of the congregation and made their statement.

With wonderful conciseness of manner, keeping themselves

strictly to facts, and coming to the point with admirable brevity, they said, "Our father died in the wilderness. He was not one of those who took part in the sin of Korah. He died quietly, not tragically. He had no sons, and according to the present law of Israel, the name of our father dies, and it is just as if he had never lived, though he has left five girls who bear his name and love his memory. Now we ask you to look at this case. It is peculiar. See if anything can be done under such extraordinary circumstances, and give us, women though we be, a possession in Israel. Give us property in the land and create a legal status for us among the brethren of our father."

To really understand and picture the effect their request caused among all the tribes of Israel, just remember the last time you went to a huge stadium and someone started "the wave." The second the daughters had finished making their unheard plea to Moses, "the wave" started from one end of the camp to the other. You can just about imagine the shock and the gamut of reactions that flew back and forth as the word spread throughout all the tribes of Israel—disbelief, anger, mockery, and probably plenty of smiles from those women in the camp who applauded Zelophehad's daughters' audacity. As the camp fires burned that day to cook their meals, there certainly was no lack for conversation.

It was a practical speech, and yet the boldness of the request started quite a novel point. As God's appointed leader, it was for Moses to say what should be done, but he did not speak on the spur of the moment. His reaction tells much about him. He did not react instantly as some of the men probably hoped he would. Instead, he demonstrated the wisdom he had learned in walking and talking with God as a friend (Exodus 33:11). He took time to consider and "brought their cause before the LORD."

The answer from heaven was: "What Zelophehad's daughters are saying is right. You must certainly give them property as an inheritance among their father's relatives and turn their father's inheritance over to them" (Numbers 27:7). Can you imagine the shocked look on the faces of the people as they stood there and heard Moses' announcement? Talk about jaws—men in particular—dropping in stunned astonishment! Just like that a new law of succession regarding land arose in Israel that day, granting the right of the family name and its inheritance to pass on to a daughter. God had honored all the women of Israel and conferred His blessing on the matters that concerned their hearts.

You have to realize that the ancient world was a man's world, but God was not bound by the dictates of societal laws either in Israel or the other cultures that had long forgotten Him and turned to false gods. He is a just and fair God. David wrote, "Righteousness and justice are the foundation of your throne" (Psalm 89:14). That day He spoke His decision through his servant Moses and gave a righteous and just decision on the matter. As Moses spoke what God had told him, it was a good reminder to all those who stood there that He had created man and woman in His image, and the blessings were not reserved just for the men. The God of Abraham, Isaac, and Jacob was just as interested in the women's well-being as the men's. It makes you wonder what kinds of conversations went on between husbands and wives that night in the thousands of tents surrounding the tabernacle.

What happened with those five women suggests that the resolution of situations that are wrong sometimes seems to come from our initiative and not from God. Look at the daughters of Zelophehad. It was the women themselves who began the reform concerning the laws of inheritance. Providence did not stir first. So it would seem on the surface of the story, and many people look at the surface and go no further, and so they blunder and often misunderstand the source of all good. Suggestions that are right and just and fair are from God. That very idea that we think is our own is not our own. It often springs from God. "Every good and perfect gift is from above, coming down from the Father of the heavenly lights" (James 1:17). He inspires the prayer that He intends to answer. He says, "Arise," when He is prepared to meet us.

An idea occurs to you, and you think it admirable and call it your own. So you change your insurance policy, enlarge your business, move to another town, strike out on another endeavor, and you think all these new changes are all your own doing. That is the fatal error. "For we are God's fellow workers" (1 Corinthians 3:9). He is the Lord of all, and all good ideas, noble impulses, holy inspirations, and sudden movements of the soul upward into higher life and broader liberty have their origin in Him. This is His plan of training His children.

He seems to stand aside and to take no part in some obviously good movement, and men say, "This is a human movement," not knowing what they are talking about—forgetting that the very idea out of which it all sprang came down from the Father of lights, that the very eloquence by which it is supported is divinely taught, that the very gold that is its strength is His. They do not go far enough back in their investigation into the origin of things, or they would find God in movements that are often credited to human genius alone.

The truth of the matter is that we do not see clearly, nor do we see all. The apostle Paul grasped this aspect of his mortality when he wrote, "For now we see through a glass, darkly; but then face to face: now I know in part; but then shall I know even as also I am known" (1 Corinthians 13:12, KJV). Because we don't see everything clearly, we are not always aware of the divine workings that are happening behind the scenes. The finest threads used to transform our lives more like Him are sometimes hidden from us by divine wisdom.

The Bible is full of the very spirit of justice. It is the Magna Charta of the civilized world. This is the spirit that gives the Bible such a wonderful hold upon the confidence of mankind. What happened to these five women and the outcome demonstrates that justice. Think of it. The ones who challenged the law were women. All the precedents of Israel up to that point leaned heavily on the expected answer to their bold appeal. In fact, I can imagine some men just waiting for Moses to put those women in their place. Why create a special law for women? Why universalize a very exceptional case? Why not put them down as sensational reformers? Yet, their case was heard with patience and answered with profound dignity.

Women, you should love the Bible! It is your friend. It has done more for you than all other books put together. Wherever it goes, it claims liberty for you, justice for you, honor for you. Repay its service by noble endeavor to make it known everywhere.

Not only were the applicants women, they were *orphans*. Their father was dead, and they had no brother to step forth and take their part to save the family name. Nothing was left them but the treasured memory of a man now dead and gone, whom they had loved. Yet the God of the universe was their friend. In front of the whole congregation, He said, "They are right." He will not break the bruised reed. The weak are as the strong before Him, and the friendless as those who are set in families. A God so just, so compassionate, so mindful of individual cases and special desires, is the God who will save the world! This God of justice is the God of love. Give any nation the Bible, and let that nation make the Bible its statute book, and every level of society will have justice: Employers will be just to their workers; workers will be just to their employers; family peace will be protected; social relations will be purified; common progress will be guaranteed. This spirit of justice is the social strength of the Bible. The small cause as well as the great is to be heard.

Some may think that this case is what may be called a secular one. It is about land and name and inheritance, and yet even that question was made a spiritual one. The Lord was King of Israel, and to the King the appeal must be made. Is Christianity farther from

God than was Judaism? Are there some questions that we now take into our own hands? Does God take no interest in our possessions, in our land, in our professions? Can He not still tell the physician what to do, the businessman what to buy, the mariner how to sail, the lawyer how to plead? In ancient Israel, with its priestly system, men had to go to the leader and the priest first. In Christianity we can go straight to God. We have no priesthood but Christ.

LIFE LESSON

Life certainly is not fair at times, and when you feel overwhelmed by the injustice of a circumstance that seems to crush you, remember that the way to the throne is open night and day. Woman, when you have been wronged and are suffering, take your situation to the Father! O man, carrying a burden too heavy for your declining strength, speak to God about the weight, and He will help you with His great power. "God is our refuge and strength, an ever-present help in trouble" (Psalm 46:1).

JOSEPH PARKER

MICAIAH

The Nobody Who Took On Two Kings and Four Hundred Prophets

Jehoshaphat replied to the king of Israel [Ahab],
"I am as you are, my people as your people, my horses
as your horses." But Jehoshaphat also said to the king of Israel,
"First seek the counsel of the LORD."

So the king of Israel brought together the prophets—
about four hundred men—and asked them, "Shall I go to war
against Ramoth Gilead, or shall I refrain?"

"Go," they answered, "for the Lord will give it into the king's hand."

But Jehoshaphat asked, "Is there not a prophet of the LORD here
whom we can inquire of?"

The king of Israel answered Jehoshaphat, "There is still one man
through whom we can inquire of the LORD, but I hate him because
he never prophesies anything good about me, but always bad.
He is Micaiah son of Imlah."

1 KINGS 22:4-8

. . . . ● ● ● ● ● . . . .

THE ALLIANCE OF KING JEHOSHAPHAT of Judah and King Ahab of Israel and their purposed recapture of the city of Ramoth Gilead from the king of Syria seemed to be a worthy cause and a no-brainer decision. Nevertheless, Jehoshaphat insisted that first they must seek the Lord. So Ahab brought together four hundred prophets whose sheer numbers and unanimous reply in favor of the attack must have been impressive. Yet it was not enough to satisfy Jehoshaphat's conscience. Even when the imagination assents to the voice of the majority, and when one's personal ambition is delighted with the confirming word of the prophets, there remains the overpowering but gracious authority of the conscience. Jehoshaphat was uneasy, notwithstanding the harmonious voice of the prophets, and asked if there was another prophet of whom they might inquire.

Ahab's reluctant concession that, yes, there was *one* more prophet, Micaiah, whom Ahab had made certain was not among the four hundred, speaks volumes about Micaiah's character. Micaiah is not one of the well-known prophets of the Old Testament such as Elijah or Jeremiah. You probably haven't even heard of this Bible nobody. This guy had courage that comes from an assurance deep down inside, and he wasn't afraid of being outnumbered by false prophets.

Ahab told Jehoshaphat that he hated Micaiah because he never prophesied anything good concerning him. Ahab had long ago closed his eyes to the light of truth and supposed that there was safety in the darkness. Rather than go to the truth teller and get at the reality of things at all cost, Ahab somehow found comfort in a huge chorus of prophetic parrots who told him exactly what he wanted to hear. Where the truth teller disturbs our peace and disappoints our ambition, we ought to learn that it is precisely at that point that we have to align ourselves with the truth. The truth teller is only powerful in proportion as he tells the truth. When he steps away from the truth, he is nothing. The power of a truth teller is simply the measure of his righteousness.

King Ahab's next tactic was to try to overawe the despised prophet with a show of pomp and circumstance as he introduced Micaiah to the royal presence. The kings were decked out in their robes at the gate of Samaria and surrounded by all the prophets prophesying for the kings to go ahead with their attack. As a singular addition to really impress Micaiah, a man named Zedekiah made Ahab horns of iron—a powerful symbolic act that was common in biblical history—and promised that "with these you will gore the Arameans until they are destroyed" (v. 11).

The deck was totally stacked in King Ahab's favor. Is it possible to find any man who dared to single-handedly oppose such unanimous testimony and overwhelming enthusiasm? The messenger who was sent to get Micaiah wished that the prophet would for once agree with the other prophets and please the king by leaving their emphatic counsel undisturbed. Thus the voice of persuasion was brought to bear forcefully upon Micaiah, and that voice is always the most difficult to resist. The temptation in this case was a double whammy. On the one hand, there was the power and the terror of the king who had sold himself to do evil and who had never held back from inflicting cruelty on those who caught the fire of his wrath. On the other hand, there was the goodwill of the messenger who wished Micaiah to escape all danger by simply pleasing the kings.

Micaiah's reply to the messenger is simply sublime: "As surely as the LORD lives, I can tell him only what the LORD tells me" (1 Kings 22:14). The humility of this answer is as conspicuous as its firmness. Its profound spirituality saves Micaiah from the allegation of being defiant. Micaiah recognizes that he is simply in the position of a servant who has nothing of his own to say, who is not called upon to invent an answer or to play the clever man in the presence of the kings. He is simply a voice that God would use for the declaration of His own will. Micaiah lives in God, for God, and has nothing of his own to calculate or consider. He will not accommodate himself to the spirit of the king's court or compromise his personal integrity and the claims of truth. As such, Micaiah is easily the most powerful man in the kingdom.

In 1 Kings 22:15-28 we see the critical moment of encounter with the kings. Micaiah's natural inclination for self-preservation would have been to seek their favor by falling in line with what they wanted to hear. But without a trace of uncertainty, Micaiah warns the kings that they should not go into battle and that certain disaster awaits them. Furthermore, he declares that the four hundred prophets were under the inspiration of a lying spirit that had specifically been sent to entice them. The leader of the prophets then strikes Micaiah on the face and taunts him with sarcasm. As a true prophet, Micaiah leaves his judgment to the decision of time. He will not stoop to argue or exchange angry words.

As was true of other enemies of King Ahab, Micaiah must pay for his fearlessness, which he undoubtedly knew before he even made his appearance before the kings. He is to be taken away to prison and fed with "the bread of affliction and water of affliction" (v. 27, KJV) until Ahab returns in peace. Micaiah then disappears from history. Of his fate we know nothing, but we have little reason to think that it was anything but a cruel death. Micaiah knows well the meaning of the king's message. Yet he calmly declares to Ahab, "If you ever return safely, the LORD has not spoken through me" (v. 28). And then he makes his appeal to the people and commits himself to the verdict of history, saying, "Mark my words, all you people!"

Micaiah's shining moment in a dark period of biblical history sets a standard for anyone who wants to live by the truth of God— it may mean that you stand completely alone in the face of ridicule. Yet Micaiah turns away proudly in the custody of his persecutors, having delivered his soul with fearlessness that did not cower or shrink even at the sight of death in its most ghastly forms. And thus it appears that Micaiah joined that elite group of men and women who have not counted their lives dear unto themselves when they were called upon to testify for truth and goodness. He stood alone to save the torch of truth from extinction and the standard of honor from overthrow.

LIFE LESSON

· · · · · · · · · · · · · · · ● ● ● ● · · · · · · · · · · · · · · ·

The kings went forth to battle, and Ahab perished without honor in the doing, having deluded himself that he could disobey God and prosper. Horsemen and chariots are nothing, gold and silver are valueless, all the resources of civilization are but an elaborate display of cobwebs. Nothing can stand in the final conflict for our souls but truth, and right, and purity. These are the eternal defenses—to these are assured complete and unchangeable victory. If God is for us, who can be against us? (Romans 8:31) And if God is against us, no matter how many kings are for us, they shall be blown away by the wind and cast away as trash. Be faithful to the voice of God and always live in the integrity of your heart.

JOSEPH PARKER

MNASON

The Nobody Who Stayed True Blue to the End

After this, we got ready and went up to Jerusalem.
Some of the disciples from Caesarea accompanied us
and brought us to the home of Mnason, where we were to stay.
He was a man from Cyprus and one of the early disciples.

ACTS 21:15-16

THERE IS SOMETHING THAT STIMULATES the imagination in the mere shadows of inconspicuous men that we meet in the New Testament story. What a strange fate that one man is to be made immortal by a single line from the Book of Acts. We do not hear another word about this host of Paul's as the apostle is returning to Jerusalem from one of his missionary trips. But if we take even these few bare words and look at them, feeling that there is someone like ourselves sketched in them, I think we get a real picture out of them and glean a lesson from this obscure man.

Mnason's name and his birthplace show that he belonged to the same class as Paul. He was a Hellenist, or a Jew by descent, but born on Gentile soil, and speaking Greek. He came from Cyprus, the native island of Barnabas, who may have been a friend of his. The verse says he was "one of the early disciples." He belonged to the original group of believers. If we interpret the Word strictly, we must suppose him to have been one of the rapidly diminishing nucleus, who thirty years or more ago had seen Christ in the flesh and been drawn to Him by His own words.

Evidently the mention of the early date of his conversion suggests that the number of his contemporaries was becoming few, and that there was a certain honor and distinction conceded by the

185

second generation of the Church to the survivors of those first converts to the Lord Jesus. Then, of course, as one of the earliest
believers, he must, by this time, have been advanced in life. A
Cypriote by birth, he had emigrated to and resided in a village on
the road to Jerusalem, and must have had the means and heart to
offer hospitality to those who needed it.

Though a Hellenist like Paul, Mnason does not seem to have
known the apostle before, for the most probable rendering of the
context is that the disciples from Caesarea, who were traveling with
Paul, "brought us to the home of Mnason," implying that this was
their first introduction to each other. But though probably unac-
quainted with the great teacher and apostle of the Gentiles—whose
ways were looked on with much doubt by many of the Palestinian
Christians—the old man, relic of the original disciples as he was,
opened his house and his heart to receive Paul.

Now if we take all of this together, the shadowy figure of Mnason
begins to become a bit more substantial and brings to light some
lessons that we would do well to take to heart.

The first thing that this old disciple says to us out of the misty
distance is: *Hold fast to your early faith, and to the Christ whom you
have known.*

Many years had passed since the days when perhaps the beauty
of the Master's own character and the sweetness of His own words
had drawn this man to Him. How much had come and gone since
then—Calvary and the Resurrection, Olivet and the Pentecost! His
eyes had seen a lot since the Son of God had walked on this earth.
His own life and mind had changed from buoyant youth to sober
old age. His whole feelings and outlook on the world were now different, for the passing of time helps to focus the lens of maturity
for those who walk with the Lord. Many of his old friends were
gone by now. James indeed was still there, and Peter and John
remained until this time, but most of the others he would have

known had died by now. A new generation was rising around him, and new thoughts and new ways were at work. But one truth remained for him what it had been in the old days, and that was the abiding of Christ in his life.

There is but one way of making all our days one, because one love, one hope, one joy, one aim binds them all together, and that is by taking the indwelling Christ for ourselves, and abiding in Him all our days as Mnason had done. Holding fast by the early convictions does not mean stiffening in them. There is plenty of room for growing in Christ. No doubt, Mnason, when he was first a disciple, knew but very little of the meaning and worth of his Master and His redemptive work, compared with what he had learned in all these years. Our true progress consists not in growing away from Jesus, but in growing up into Him (Ephesians 4:15), not in passing through life and leaving behind our first convictions of Him as Savior, but in having these verified by the experience of years, deepened and cleared, unfolded and ordered into a larger, though still incomplete, whole.

Mnason truly is one of the most obscure people in the Book of Acts, but he is a beautiful example of one who is not famous, below whose feet time is crumbling away, still holding firmly by faith to the Lord whom he has loved and served all his days. This small and seemingly insignificant disciple exhorts us all to remain faithful to the Lord. Whether we are just beginning our walk of faith or near the end of our race, Mnason would say to us, "Cast not away therefore your confidence, which hath great recompense of reward" (Hebrews 10:35, KJV). We are to continue to grow in grace as the years pass us by.

It is evidently meant that we should take notice of Mnason's position and reputation in the local church as significant in regard to his hospitable reception of the apostle Paul. It is conceivable to assume that the little knot of "original disciples" would have been apt to value themselves on their position, especially as time went on and their ranks were thinned. Perhaps they were tempted to believe that they understood the Master's meaning a great deal better than those who had never known Christ personally. And no doubt they possibly shared in the suspicion that many of the Jewish party held toward Paul. Because of the persecution he had carried out toward believers before his conversion, not everyone totally trusted him yet (Acts 26:1-12).

It would have been very natural for this good old man to have said, "I do not like these new-fangled ways. There was nothing of this sort in my younger days. Is it not likely that we, who were at the beginning of the Gospel, should understand the Gospel and the Church's work without this new man coming to set us right? I am too old to go in with these changes." All the more honorable is it that Mnason was willing and ready with an open house to shelter the great champion of the Gentile churches—and, as we may reasonably believe, welcome Paul's teaching with an open heart. Change is hard for anyone, and not every "old disciple" would have been so accommodating.

Mnason's flexibility of mind and openness of nature to welcome new ways of work, united with the persistent constancy in his old creed, make an admirable combination. It is rare enough at any age, but especially in elderly believers. We would do well to try to imitate the persistency and open mind of that "old disciple" who was so ready to welcome and entertain the apostle of the Gentile Church.

There is still another lesson, and that is the beauty that may dwell in an obscure life. There is nothing to be said about this old man but that he was a disciple. He had done no great thing for his Lord that is recorded. He was not renowned as a teacher or preacher, nor is he known for his eloquence or genius. No great heroic deed or piece of saintly endurance is recorded of him. But the few words mentioned—"one of the early disciples"—is very significant: He had loved and followed Christ all his days. And so Mnason did what he could do. He graciously opened his house for Paul and his company, and in doing so, he shared in the apostle's work. The Scriptures say, "Anyone who receives a prophet because he is a prophet will receive a prophet's reward, and anyone who receives a righteous man because he is a righteous man will receive a righteous man's reward" (Matthew 10:41). He who with understanding and sympathy welcomes and sustains the prophet aligns himself with the righteous workings of the Lord.

His life cries from afar off, "Grow in grace and in the knowledge of Him, whom to know ever so imperfectly is eternal life, whom to know a little better is the true progress for men, whom to know more and more fully is the growth and gladness and glory of the heavens. So with purpose of heart, remain faithful to the Lord."

LIFE LESSON

D o you ever wonder if the work you have been called to do for God is even noticed? Remember Mnason, for this old disciple's hospitality was immortalized, and the record of it reminds us that the smallest service done for Jesus is remembered and treasured by Him. Do not seek great things for yourself, but rather fill every corner of your life with the unnoticed work of love for your Lord. Pay no attention to whether the world remembers your service or praises it. But be sure that Christ Himself takes notice, whose praise is the only fame, and whose remembrance is the highest reward. God is not unrighteous to forget your work and labor of love.

ALEXANDER MACLAREN

MORDECAI

The Nobody Who Outfoxed the Fox

*Now there was in the citadel of Susa a Jew of the tribe of Benjamin,
named Mordecai son of Jair, the son of Shimei, the son of Kish,
who had been carried into exile from Jerusalem by Nebuchadnezzar
king of Babylon, among those taken captive with Jehoiachin king
of Judah. Mordecai had a cousin named Hadassah, whom he had
brought up because she had neither father nor mother. This girl,
who was also known as Esther, was lovely in form and features,
and Mordecai had taken her as his own daughter
when her father and mother died.*

ESTHER 2:5-7

. . . . ● ● ● ● ● . . . .

THE HISTORICAL EVENTS SURROUNDING the story of Mordecai—only one of thousands of unknown Jews taken into captivity—take place in one of the most powerful kingdoms of the Middle East—Persia—under the rule of Xerxes. To better understand some of the lessons that we see in the Book of Esther, it is necessary to understand, in part, the history of the Jews and how they ended up living so far from the Promised Land.

About 103 years earlier, Nebuchadnezzar, king of Babylon, had carried off the Jews into captivity because of their unfaithfulness to God (2 Chronicles 36:15-21). For years God had warned them through the prophets to return to Him, "but they mocked God's messengers, despised his words and scoffed at his prophets until the wrath of the LORD was aroused against his people and there was no remedy" (v. 16). Judgment finally came, and God gave them over to the king of Babylon.

But as it goes with all empires, Babylon's rule came to an end when the Persians conquered Babylon in 539 B.C. Yet even despite the years God's people were held in Babylon as captives, His divine will was still working on the course of human events. God moved upon Cyrus's heart in a sovereign act: "In order to fulfill the word of the LORD spoken by Jeremiah, the LORD *moved the heart* of Cyrus king of Persia to make a proclamation" (vv. 22-23, emphasis added). That proclamation was about the return of the Jews to their land and a direct fulfillment of a prophecy by Jeremiah years earlier.

Divine wisdom never lacks for someone to witness of the one true God. And such was the case with Cyrus. Though advanced in years, the prophet Daniel was still alive and receiving his divine revelations at the beginning of Cyrus's reign (Daniel 10:1). Surely the events of Daniel's interpretations of Nebuchadnezzar's dreams (Daniel 2; 4) and the writing on the wall when judgment came to King Belshazzar (Daniel 5) were known by Cyrus. It was common for ancient rulers to keep annals filled with details of the major events that took place in their kingdoms. Daniel was held in such high esteem throughout his life with the Babylonians that he would have had some influence on Cyrus's knowledge of the God of the Jews.

Cyrus's proclamation declares what God had revealed to him: "The LORD, the God of heaven, has given me all the kingdoms of the earth and he has appointed me to build a temple for him at Jerusalem in Judah. Anyone of his people among you—may the LORD his God be with him, and let him go up" (v. 23). God was going to use Cyrus to begin the rebuilding of the temple at Jerusalem, which required him to allow the Jews to finally return to their land.

Under the rule of Cyrus, and after this amazing edict, the Jewish exiles could either choose to return to their homeland or remain. Many chose to return to Jerusalem. But after so many years of captivity, a number of them had become established in their own lives and business throughout the Persian empire. They had gained more freedoms under the Persians than as captives under

Nebuchadnezzar's rule. The trip back over the desert to Jerusalem was a long and dangerous one, and some Jews did not want to risk the trip. Mordecai's family was one who had chosen to remain.

Mordecai was of the tribe of Benjamin and lived in Susa, the capital of the Persian empire, around 483 B.C. during the reign of Xerxes, also known as Ahasuerus. This was about fifty-four years after Zerubbabel had led the first group of exiles back to Jerusalem (Ezra 1; 2). Now Mordecai had a cousin by the name of Hadassah, whom he had raised as his own daughter because her parents were dead. Hadassah is also known as Esther, who was chosen above all the lovely maidens of the empire to become queen when Xerxes banished Queen Vashti from his presence for refusing to appear before him on the occasion of a royal banquet in front of all the noble lords of the kingdom.

Mordecai was a noble man of devout faith and cared for Esther as his own, yet he had forbidden her to reveal her nationality. The Jews had been brought back as captives by the Babylonians a century before and suffered at the hands of their captors. Perhaps in wisdom he had kept their Jewish heritage a secret to avoid being taunted, reviled, and disgraced. Though he kept their nationality a secret, he raised Esther by the Law of Moses. He passed on to her the faith of his fathers, instructing her in the ways of the one true God.

Suddenly, Mordecai's world is turned upside down when Esther is crowned the new queen by King Xerxes. Yet out of fatherly concern, he walks "back and forth near the courtyard of the harem to find out how Esther was and what was happening to her" (Esther 2:11). His is a large heart filled with love for her, and as he walks outside the king's gate, he must have pondered why divine providence had allowed Esther to become queen of the most powerful kingdom at that time. Yet even as queen, Esther still listens to Mordecai's wisdom. In deference and obedience to him, Esther keeps her family background and nationality a secret (Esther 2:20).

On a certain day, Mordecai is sitting at the king's gate and learns of a assassination plot by Bigthana and Teresh, two of the king's officers, who are conspiring to kill King Xerxes. He reports the plot to Queen Esther, who in turn informs the king. The king's life is saved and the credit is given to Mordecai (2:22). The details are even recorded in the book of the annals in the presence of the king.

We also see the depth of Mordecai's faith when he refuses to kneel down and honor Haman, whom King Xerxes had appointed to a high government position: "All the royal officials at the king's gate knelt down and paid honor to Haman, for the king had commanded this concerning him. But Mordecai would not kneel down or pay him honor" (Esther 3:2). In obedience to the second commandment given by Moses on Mount Sinai (Exodus 5), Mordecai would rather place his life in danger than disobey God and bow down to a mere mortal. You can rest assured that as a Jew, he had heard of the courageous act of obedience years before by Shadrach, Meshach, and Abednego (Daniel 3). Their God, who had delivered them from the fiery furnace, was the same God Mordecai worshiped. He decided to trust the outcome of his obedience to a higher law of justice.

Yet sometimes our obedience to a higher law stirs the wrath of those who do not understand God's ways. Such was the case with Mordecai and Haman. The text says that the royal officials spoke with Mordecai day after day, but "he refused to comply" and kneel down to Haman (Esther 3:4). He told them he was a Jew, and in so doing, he surely would have explained to them why he was forbidden to bow down to Haman.

"When Haman saw that Mordecai would not kneel down or pay him honor, he was enraged" (Esther 3:5). Isn't that the way with inflated egos? The more they are ignored, the more they fume in rage and try to seek revenge. Have you ever felt the surge of anger rise inside you when people do not give you the respect you think you deserve? In our modern twenty-first-century culture, we still expect a certain "bowing down" in how people treat us. We want to be addressed with a certain title that strokes our elevated view of ourselves. We want that certain seat during business meetings so we can command everyone's attention. We want preferential treatment in all areas of our life, both personal and professional.

And when people don't "bow down" to our expectations and honor us, we become enraged. With some that anger explodes, while others of us use more refined ways to seek our revenge than Haman did. But evil is evil, whether it happened thousands of years ago in a royal Persian court, or occurs in an executive board meeting where CEOs plot to save their investments and leave the little guy in the lurch when a company begins to crumble because of dishonesty. Little natures require great revenge. Little natures endeavor to magnify themselves by exaggeration.

Haman not only construed a plan to kill Mordecai, he used his power and influence to manipulate Xerxes to issue an irrevocable edict to slay a group of people—the Jews—who Haman said had different customs and did not obey Xerxes' laws (Esther 3:8-9). Haman's hatred would have every Jewish man, woman, and child slain to appease his offended ego. He even went so far as to offer "ten thousand talents of silver into the royal treasury for the men who carry out this business" (Esther 3:9).

When Mordecai learned of the edict, he "tore his clothes, put on sackcloth and ashes, and went out into the city, wailing loudly and bitterly" (Esther 4:1). His mourning was noticed by all, and word was soon brought to Queen Esther by her maids and eunuchs. She immediately sent a messenger to find out what was troubling Mordecai.

Even though thousands of years of history have gone by, God is still God, and He is never caught by surprise by those who plot wickedness. Mordecai's and Esther's lives are a faith-inspiring testimony of the fact that God always has His right people in the right place at the right time. Mordecai sends word back to the queen and pleads for her to intervene on behalf of all the Jews. His plea is a marvelous example of someone who, like Moses, gave himself to interceding for his people. But Esther sends word to Mordecai that to approach the king when he had not summoned her could be punishable by death (Esther 4:11).

Mordecai's reply to Esther's concern answers a question everyone asks at some time in their lives. Why am I where I'm at, and what purpose does my life fulfill? For those who walk in the ways of righteousness, the Lord has His men and women well placed to thwart the plans of evil. Mordecai's question to Esther reveals God's working in human history, one of the main themes of this whole story: "Who knows but that you have come to royal position for such a time as this?" (Esther 4:14)

We get another glimpse of Mordecai's godly character when he wholeheartedly agrees to Esther's request to seek God in humility and fasting with all the Jews (Esther 4:15-17) as she courageously agrees to approach the king. She uses wisdom in how she reveals Haman's wicked scheme (Esther 7).

Even when the king honors Mordecai for having uncovered an assassination plot, Haman continues to seethe with anger at what he considers a gross injustice. But wickedness knows nothing of justice or humility and lays a snare for its own feet by the blindness that surrounds it. David wrote: "The LORD is known by his justice; the wicked are ensnared by the work of their hands" (Psalm 9:16).

Haman becomes ensnared by his pride and wickedness, is discovered, and is hanged on the very gallows he had intended for Mordecai (Esther 7:10). King Xerxes cannot revoke the edict, but he grants permission for the Jews to defend themselves on the appointed day they are to be destroyed. Xerxes then gives all of Haman's estate to Esther. She tells the king of Mordecai's relationship to her, and

Xerxes takes off his signet ring of power that he had reclaimed from Haman and gives it to Mordecai (Esther 8:1-3).

Mordecai's life is a demonstration of how God can use anyone, anytime, anywhere if they will be faithful in the place God has placed them.

LIFE LESSON

Do you feel that the Hamans of your life have the upper hand? Do you ask yourself why you are where you're at in life? Remember that every child of God is where God has placed them for some purpose. When the problems of life seem too much, look up as the psalmist did and declare: "My help comes from the Lord, the Maker of heaven and earth" (Psalm 121:2). God will not abandon us where He has placed us. Our job is to discover His purpose and fulfill it as Mordecai did. We are to serve Jesus exactly where we are as a living example of His truth. Do not spend your days filled with jealousy and complaining about your lot in life. God's ability to work His perfect will in your life is just as powerful today in the twenty-first century as it was thousands of years ago in the court of a Persian king. Do not forget the fact that God in His providence places His servants in positions where He can make the best use of them. Only be faithful to Him where you are, and in His good time you will have both His blessing and His reward.

JOSEPH PARKER

NABOTH
the JEZREELITE

The Nobody Who Wasn't About to Give Up His Vineyard

Some time later there was an incident involving a vineyard belonging to Naboth the Jezreelite. The vineyard was in Jezreel, close to the palace of Ahab king of Samaria. Ahab said to Naboth, "Let me have your vineyard to use for a vegetable garden, since it is close to my palace. In exchange I will give you a better vineyard or, if you prefer, I will pay you whatever it is worth."

But Naboth replied, "The LORD forbid that I should give you the inheritance of my fathers."

So Ahab went home, sullen and angry. . . .

1 KINGS 21:1-4

. . . . ● ● ● ● ● . . . .

ONCE UPON A TIME, on a small vineyard located on the eastern slope of the hill of Jezreel during the reign of the villainous King Ahab and the devilish Queen Jezebel lived a man named Naboth. He appeared to be an ordinary man whose only noteworthy possession was his vineyard. Had he not lived so close to the royal palace and the dark scrutiny of Ahab, I would not be writing about him and his sons today. But when the king, who already had immeasurable possessions, turned his envious eye upon that fine vineyard, Naboth became the focus and target of devouring covetousness.

King Ahab, on the other hand, was anything but an ordinary man. About him we are told these remarkable words: "(There was never a man like Ahab, who sold himself to do evil in the eyes of the LORD, urged on by Jezebel his wife. He behaved in the vilest manner by going after idols, like the Amorites the LORD drove out before Israel)" (1 Kings 21:25-26). This is not the sort of fellow you would want to have as your neighbor, and his wife was even worse, but such was Naboth's position in life.

From a business perspective, the financial terms offered to Naboth do not appear to be unreasonable or unacceptable. The king's approach was courteous and clear—neither of which were characteristic of the king's other dealings. He simply wished to purchase the vineyard or to open negotiations concerning a trade for an even better vineyard somewhere else. Given Ahab's ruthless ways, it appears that Naboth should take the cash and run. There's nothing apparently unscrupulous going on here. Just a wealthy man offering a poor nobody a good deal. Right? Wrong.

Naboth possessed the vineyard Ahab is said to have coveted. His response to Ahab, "The LORD forbid . . . ," was born of deep certainty. Naboth made a spiritual issue out of it. Why did he invoke the Eternal Name and stand back as if an offense had been offered to his faith? The reason is that Naboth had inherited the vineyard from his fathers, and no Israelite could lawfully sell his property (Leviticus 25:23; Numbers 36:7; Ezekiel 46:18). So Naboth was merely standing upon the law, which in this case was the law of God, answering solemnly and spiritually. There was no haughtiness or resentfulness or defiance in Naboth's response.

When money was offered for his fathers' inheritance, Naboth spurned the request. There are some things, blessed be God, we cannot pay for. When Ahab suggested he could give Naboth a better vineyard, he obviously had no idea what he was talking about. There can be no better vineyard than the vineyard of your fathers. There can be no vineyard equal to the vineyard that is sown in history, planted with family and friends, celebrated and endeared by a thousand precious memories. Surely there are some things we should never be willing to sell. Truly, when we hear propositions that money or something else will be given to us in exchange for certain things, we need to weigh carefully what it may cost our soul. Any offer that compromises our relationship with God will injure our whole soul and must be rejected at its very approach.

So Naboth took a strong position in the will of God, and he had the courage to answer the king in those terms. Kings must submit to law. Kings ought to be the subjects of their own people in this regard. Ahab was taught that there was at least one man in Samaria who valued the inheritance handed down to him and would not bend the knee to violate God's command. Have we no inheritance handed down to us—no Word of God, no gospel that has set our heart free, no standard of morality that is as firm as the heavens? Do we inherit nothing? Are we not bound to hand on to others the sacred truths that have been born in our lives?

Naboth refused to compromise, though he knew that Jezebel would never let it pass. Living in the shadows of the palace, he was aware that her evil spirit always found ways of obtaining whatever she wanted. The spilling of innocent blood had never satiated her wicked heart. By a crafty and cruel plot that was cloaked with a religious fast, truth would be ceremoniously trampled under foot (1 Kings 21:8-14). A great black lie was loosed to pervert others' minds and purposefully mislead. And in short order, Naboth and his sons were taken outside the city and stoned to death (2 Kings 9:26).

Naboth perished for a righteous stand, but God immediately validated him. Ahab had no sooner gone down to take possession of the vineyard when the prophet Elijah suddenly appeared and pronounced against him a divine message of retribution for the innocent man's murder (1 Kings 21:17-24). Ahab had pushed the divine patience and forbearing past its final limit, and Ahab and Jezebel were about to pay the price.

Better, indeed, is a little vineyard on a rocky hill that a righteous man has than the richest estate of the wicked.

LIFE LESSON

· · · · · · · · · · · · · · · · · ● ● ● · · · · · · · · · · · · · · · ·

Like Naboth, we are called to greater things than this world can offer. Never take whatever the world offers as a substitute for the life you received in the Lord Jesus Christ. You have an inheritance in heaven that is incorruptible and undefiled and unfading (1 Peter 1:4-5). Crush the very beginnings of evil. Resist the beginnings. Live as a trustee of the sacred possessions God has given you and bind yourself to vindicate that trust.

JOSEPH PARKER

OBADIAH

The Nobody Who Kept Pure in a Cesspool

*After a long time, in the third year, the word of the LORD came to
Elijah: "Go and present yourself to Ahab, and I will send rain
on the land." So Elijah went to present himself to Ahab.*

*Now the famine was severe in Samaria, and Ahab had summoned
Obadiah, who was in charge of his palace. (Obadiah was a devout
believer in the Lord. While Jezebel was killing off the LORD's prophets,
Obadiah had taken a hundred prophets and hidden them in two
caves, fifty in each, and had supplied them with food and water.)
Ahab had said to Obadiah, "Go through the land to all the springs
and valleys. Maybe we can find some grass to keep the horses and
mules alive so we will not have to kill any of our animals."
So they divided the land they were to cover,
Ahab going in one direction and Obadiah in another.*

1 KINGS 18:1-6

. . . . ● ● ● ● . . . .

THIS OBADIAH (for there are others of the name mentioned in the Old Testament) lived in the reign of Ahab, king of Israel. Obadiah was a servant, a nobody whose sole job was to serve the needs of the king. It was an evil time. Ahab, we read, "did more evil in the eyes of the LORD than any of those before him" (1 Kings 16:30). After his marriage with Jezebel, a heathen princess, he went to yet greater lengths of evil than before. He himself worshiped Baal, a Canaanite fertility deity, and built Baal a house, and set him up an altar, and made an idolatrous grove. Again we read, "Ahab . . . did more to provoke the LORD, the God of Israel, to anger than did all the kings of Israel before him" (1 Kings 16:33).

The people were not slow to follow such a leading. The number of the prophets of Baal shows the widespread prevalence of idolatry. There were four hundred fifty of them. Yet in that evil time the Lord had those who were His. Even when Elijah complained to the Lord and said only he remained loyal, the Lord told him that seven thousand had not bowed the knee to Baal. They were hidden among the overwhelming crowd of idolaters, but the Lord knew them.

In all the kingdom there was not a more unlikely place for a righteous man to be found than in the house of Ahab. Yet *there* in the house of the most wicked king of all Israel lived at least one of those seven thousand. Obadiah, Ahab's chief servant, the governor of his house, was no idolater, but one who was "a devout believer in the Lord" (1 Kings 18:3). His name Obadiah, meaning "a servant of the Lord," was a true description of him.

No time, however evil, and no circumstances, however unfavorable, can make it impossible to serve God. Obadiah, though set over the king's household, was but a servant. Yet as a servant in an ungodly and idolatrous household, he lived as one who "feared the LORD greatly" (v. 3, KJV). It is plain that these words describe not only his inward feelings but also his outward life and conduct. He had feared the Lord from his youth, and probably then also in the household of Ahab; growing up in that wicked family as a godly young man, he had advanced from one post to another, until he became the governor of the house.

One particular instance shows us Obadiah's God-fearing character. The wicked queen, Jezebel, was not only an idolater, but also a cruel persecutor. When she first became queen, there were many prophets of the Lord, teachers of true religion, scattered throughout the land of Israel, but she set herself to destroy them all. During a violent persecution that she raised against them, Obadiah showed his commitment to God. He could not stop the persecution, but he could save some of the prophets from it. He saved no less than a hundred of these prophets of the Lord. He hid them in a cave and fed them with bread and water, a great risk to himself. No doubt his position in Ahab's house was of great influence and usefulness, which enabled him to protect the prophets. And doubtless many other opportunities to do good came to him in his daily life as steward of the house.

The servants of God are not to think of their own comfort alone. True, they are not willfully to choose their place in life among the ungodly, and thus run the risk of spiritual loss to themselves. But a position of usefulness, in which a person finds himself through the providence of God, is not lightly to be given up because of discomfort and lack of spiritual fellowship. Much watchfulness and prayer are needed in such a situation.

But how did Ahab keep such a God-fearing steward? We can well believe that Jezebel was vehemently against him, and for Ahab himself it might have been more agreeable to have a chief servant like-minded with himself. Yet we find Obadiah, who "feared the Lord greatly," serving as steward to the wicked king of Israel.

A wicked man knows whom he can trust. Many an ungodly master is glad to have a servant who fears God. A proof of this trust was given by Ahab when he sent Obadiah to search the land for grass and water, for the cattle were perishing from the severe drought Elijah had prophesied. They divided the land between them. Ahab went one way, and Obadiah went another.

While carrying out the king's command, Obadiah was met by Elijah. Three years before, the prophet had appeared before Ahab and told him, in the name of the Lord, that there would be no dew or rain, unless commanded by his word or prayer. The king became furious, and during the severe famine that followed, Ahab looked for Elijah everywhere, but without success. Elijah had fled at God's command and still continued to prophesy under His protection and support. But a new command had now come to Elijah to go to Ahab and announce that the Lord would send rain. It was to Obadiah that the prophet first showed himself, meeting Ahab's servant as he went through the land on his search. Elijah commanded Obadiah to deliver his message to Ahab.

But Obadiah foresaw danger in this service. He believed that Elijah was a prophet, and that he was under the special protection of God. He felt sure that Elijah's many escapes from Ahab up to that moment had been through God's care over the prophet. And now he feared that the prophet did not really mean to show himself to the king. Obadiah was afraid that the Spirit of the Lord would whisk him away, and when Ahab came and found him gone, he would vent his wrath on Obadiah and slay him as a deceiver (1 Kings 18:8-14).

There appears to be a mixture of faith and unbelief in Obadiah, which may appear strange, but it is by no means uncommon. Obadiah seems to have had faith for another, but not for himself. He felt sure that God would continue to preserve Elijah. Before Ahab could come to the place, the prophet would again have been carried to some safe refuge, beyond the reach of the king. But would the Lord care for the safety of one faithful servant, and yet leave another to perish? So Obadiah seemed to fear that Elijah would be rescued, but *he* would be slain.

Faith, even when true, often shows itself weak and inconsistent. It will believe a part, but not all. Obadiah reminded Elijah of his own good deed of hiding the prophets, though it is most likely that Elijah knew of it. But he did so in no vain or self-righteous spirit. He was not boasting, but making a humble request. He wished to prove himself a true servant of God, and no idolater, and desired to be treated as such, and as such to be acknowledged by the prophet. Obadiah said, "Yet I your servant have worshiped the LORD since my youth" (v. 12). This was but a profession of faith, such as all believers are bound to make, especially in an ungodly age like that.

Elijah gave Obadiah a positive promise that he would show himself to Ahab that day, and then Obadiah feared no more. Prophet met king, and Ahab did nothing against him, nor did Obadiah suffer any harm. Thus the Lord preserved them both.

LIFE LESSON

W e should seek to be strong in faith, for even in the midst of the most evil circumstances you can hold fast to your godly convictions and be a true servant of the living God. When you feel assailed on all sides by doubt and anxiety, it is in those moments that God delights to visit His children and say, "I will surely bless, I will surely save, I will surely guide." Let us meet every difficulty and danger, trusting in His Word. Obadiah was quite safe, and so is every prayerful, trusting, obedient servant of God.

FRANCIS BOURDILLON

OBED-EDOM
the GITTITE

The Nobody Who Got Blessed Out of His Socks

David was afraid of the LORD *that day and said, "How can the ark of the* LORD *ever come to me?" He was not willing to take the ark of the* LORD *to be with him in the City of David. Instead, he took it aside to the house of Obed-Edom the Gittite. The ark of the* LORD *remained in the house of Obed-Edom the Gittite for three months, and the* LORD *blessed him and his entire household.*

Now King David was told, "The LORD *has blessed the household of Obed-Edom and everything he has, because of the ark of God." So David went down and brought up the ark of God from the house of Obed-Edom to the City of David with rejoicing.*

2 SAMUEL 6:9-12

· ● ● ● ● ·

T HE ARK WAS THE SYMBOL, or sign, of God's presence with the Israelites. It was made by God's command, and by His command it was to be treated with reverence. When it was disassembled and moved from place to place, there were very explicit procedures that had to be followed to the letter of the Law literally. The priests were first to cover it, and then the Levites of one particular family, the Kohathites, were to carry it, but without touching the Ark itself. They were to touch the staves, and possibly the covering, only. This sacredness was not a superstitious sacredness, a thing of man's invention, but a real sanctity given to the Ark by God Himself (Numbers 4).

Throughout their wanderings through the wilderness, the Ark was a physical manifestation for the Israelites—as well as the nations around them—that God was with them. At one point in their history, their enemies, the Philistines, won a crucial battle and captured the Ark (1 Samuel 4:10-11). They took the Ark of God from Ebenezer to Ashdod. They had seen the power the Ark had given to the Israelites, and they wanted it for themselves, for they had seen the victories the Israelites had won because of the Ark's presence in their camp. They did not see it as the symbol of a living God who wanted to make His presence known, but rather as a trophy of power they could manipulate and use to their own military advantage.

So after capturing it, "they carried the ark into Dagon's temple and set it beside Dagon. When the people of Ashdod rose early the next day, there was Dagon, fallen on his face on the ground before the ark of the Lord!" (1 Samuel 5:2-4) They stood him back in place, but the next morning he had fallen again. But this time, his head and hands had been broken off (v. 4).

Dagon was the chief god of the Philistines, though they worshiped many other ones as well. They believed that Dagon was responsible for blessing them with abundant rain so that they would have a bountiful harvest. But there is but one God that men are to worship, and He will not share His glory with another: "I am the LORD; that is my name! I will not give my glory to another or my praise to idols" (Isaiah 42:8). To place the Ark of God next to a pagan idol was a serious abomination, and the Scriptures say, "The LORD's hand was heavy upon the people of Ashdod and its vicinity; he brought devastation upon them and afflicted them with tumors" (1 Samuel 5:6). It didn't take them very long to realize that "the ark of the god of Israel" (v. 7) wasn't delivering all they had anticipated. So the rulers got together and decided to move it to Gath. But the same judgment fell on that city as well, and many died from tumors and a plague brought on by rats. When they tried to take it to a third city, the inhabitants of Ekron cried out for fear that they would all die (v. 10). Finally, the Philistines called together all their rulers and decided to send it back to Israel. After much consultation with their priests and diviners, they decided to send it back with a guilt offering.

The priests said they had to send it back with "five gold tumors and five gold rats, according to the number of the Philistine rulers" (1 Samuel 6:5). Their guilt offering represented the two plagues—tumors and rats—that had come upon them and were destroying them. Placing the Ark on a new cart with two cows, they sent it off. They told themselves that if the cows went straight toward Israel, then they would know that what had come upon them had been by the hand of God (1 Samuel 6:7-12). The cows went straight up toward Beth Shemesh. When the Israelites saw it, the people chopped up the cart and sacrificed the cows as a burnt offering to the Lord (v. 15).

God had to remind His people of the seriousness of His holiness because of the disrespect shown by certain men of Beth Shemesh. He had commanded the people through Moses not to even look at the holy objects that had been placed in the Holy of Holies or they would die (Numbers 4:20). Despite God's clear rule, seventy men looked into the Ark of the Lord, and they all were struck down by God. Because of the severe judgment, the people of Beth Shemesh called the men of Kiriath Jearim to come and take the Ark: "They took it to Abinadab's house on the hill and consecrated Eleazar his son to guard the ark of the LORD" (1 Samuel 7:1).

When David became king, the Ark had been in the house of Abinadab at Kiriath Jearim for twenty years. David had not long been settled on the throne of Israel, when he determined to bring the Ark to Jerusalem. He gathered together, therefore, all the chosen men of Israel, no less than 30,000 in number, in order to pay honor to the Ark of God (2 Samuel 6:1-6). The distance was short, and they were probably near to Jerusalem when their journey suddenly came to a stop. Uzzah and Ahio, the sons of Abinadab, were driving the cart. They were certainly not priests, and it does not appear that they were even Levites. When the oxen that drew the cart stumbled, Uzzah reached out and took hold of the Ark to steady it. An awful judgment followed: "The LORD's anger burned against Uzzah because of his irreverent act; therefore God struck him down and he died there beside the ark of God" (v. 7). The text says that David became angry and afraid, and decided he didn't want to bring the Ark to Jerusalem.

This incident caused a great change in the mind of David. Thus far he and all the people had accompanied the Ark with joy and praise and exultation, playing on harps, lyres, tambourines, sistrums, and cymbals (2 Samuel 6:5). But it says that David was angry, and a fear came over him. This fear does not seem to have been a believing and reverential fear, such as Uzzah should have had, which would have prevented his death, but what comes over David is an unreasoning and unbelieving dread. And so the Ark was stopped in its journey to Jerusalem and carried aside into the house of Obed-Edom.

And who was Obed-Edom? And where was his house? Obed-Edom was a Levite. This is plain from several places in the first Book of Chronicles. There he is mentioned as one of the porters, or guards of the sanctuary, and also as a player on the harp, and further as one of the gatekeepers for the Ark (1 Chronicles 15:18, 21, 24). To this last post of honor, however, he seems to have been appointed after the resting of the Ark in his house, and probably because he had taken care of it with the respect prescribed by the Law of Moses. He is called Obed-Edom the Gittite. It is probable that he was from Gath-rimmon, situated in the tribe of Dan, one of the cities allotted to the Kohathites, one of the families of the Levites. Now, from the fact that he was appointed one of the gatekeepers of the Ark, it seems likely that Obed-Edom was of the Kohathites, whose particular office it was to bear the Ark. This Levite city,

Gath-rimmon, therefore was probably either his birthplace or his dwelling place, and that is why he was called the Gittite.

Where the house of Obed-Edom was we do not know. Possibly it was at Gath-rimmon itself. Though it was not in the direct route from Kiriath Jearim to Jerusalem, the place could not have been very far out of the way because it says that David "took it aside to the house of Obed-Edom" (2 Samuel 6:10). David carried the Ark into the house of Obed-Edom, and it was readily received. We must not suppose that Obed-Edom had no choice in the matter. If he had received it merely because David brought it, and if he had kept it in his house only as he would have obeyed any other command of the king, then it is not likely that he would have received such an honorable mention. He received the Ark willingly, and his conduct stands out in contrast to the anger that David had displayed.

If there was danger to David and his house from the Ark, was the danger less to Obed-Edom? If David said, "How can the ark of the LORD ever come to me?" might not Obed-Edom have said the same? He surely would have been aware of the terrible judgment that had fallen on Uzzah. Most likely it had happened close to his house. And if not, such news would have traveled fast. Those who came to his house with the Ark would not fail to tell him what had happened to Uzzah. Now, knowing all that had happened, and seeing the fear on every face, and well aware of the strong feelings that led David to take the Ark aside to his house, Obed-Edom did not decline to undertake the awesome responsibility.

As a Levite, and probably of the family of Kohath, he knew the fault that Uzzah had been guilty of, and saw in his death only the just punishment for disobeying an express command passed down from Moses regarding the sanctity of the Ark. Because Obed-Edom received the sacred symbol of God's presence with all reverence, and was prepared to treat it exactly according to the command of God, he was not afraid of being visited with the same fate. Rather, he thought it an honor to be responsible for the Ark, and in faith and thankfulness, he opened his house to take in the Ark of God.

The Ark remained in his house for three months. The presence of the Lord, of which the Ark was the symbol, brought a blessing with it, for the Bible says, ". . . the LORD blessed him and his entire household" (v. 11). Everything about Obed-Edom and his house were blessed, and in no small way. So obvious was the blessing that all men noticed it and spoke of it. Everyone saw that the Lord's hand was in it—all traced to the presence of the Ark in his house. And so word of it spread back to Jerusalem, and King David was told, "The LORD has blessed the household of Obed-Edom and everything he has, because of the ark of God" (v. 12). So David, finally convinced that the Ark brought good and not evil, "went down and brought up the ark of God from the house of Obed-Edom to the City of David with rejoicing" (v. 12).

Thus, after a stay of three months, the Ark was gone from the house of Obed-Edom. But the blessing that it had brought did not depart when the Ark was taken to Jerusalem. Long after, we read of his sons and his sons' sons as numbering sixty-two in all, "leaders," "capable men with the strength to do the work" of gatekeepers (1 Chronicles 26:1-9). At the end of this genealogy of Obed-Edom, who had eight sons, we find an interesting verse that sums up all that God had done for him: "For God had blessed Obed-Edom" (v. 5). Because it comes at the end of the genealogy, we know that God's blessing had given Obed-Edom a rich heritage in his children and grandchildren. And those descendants were gifted as leaders and capable men to continue the work of keeping the Ark. The blessing was continued long after the Ark was gone, for God's presence did not depart when the outward symbol of it was removed. His presence and blessing are not tied to any outward signs or means.

We never hear of this man until the Ark comes to his house.

And the service to which he was called, compared with the service of some, seems but a humble service—to take charge of the Ark for three months. Yet because of his faithfulness to obey the instructions on how to treat the Ark with respect, he and his descendants were blessed for years.

LIFE LESSON

The Lord who blessed Obed-Edom and his house will likewise bless every such household. God blesses His servants, and accepts what they do, not for their high position or for the greatness of the work they are called to, but for their character in His sight—their faith, their love, their zeal—and for the way in which they do what they are called to be, be it much or little. Obed-Edom entertained the Ark in his house and found a blessing from it. We have the privilege of becoming temples of the living God—His Spirit dwelling within us—so let us entertain the Lord Himself in our hearts so that we truly become temples of the Holy Spirit. Then a richer blessing will be ours. God is graciously willing to make His abode with us. "For this is what the high and lofty One says—he who lives forever, whose name is holy: 'I live in a high and holy place, but also with him who is contrite and lowly in spirit, to revive the spirit of the lowly and to revive the heart of the contrite' " (Isaiah 57:15).

FRANCIS BORDILLON

ONESIMUS, a RUNAWAY SLAVE

The Nobody Who Returned a Changed Man

*I appeal to you for my son Onesimus, who became my son
while I was in chains. Formerly he was useless to you,
but now he has become useful both to you and to me.*

*I am sending him—who is my very heart—back to you.
I would have liked to keep him with me so that he could take
your place in helping me while I am in chains for the gospel.
But I did not want to do anything without your consent, so that
any favor you do will be spontaneous and not forced. Perhaps the
reason he was separated from you for a little while was that you
might have him back for good—no longer as a slave, but better
than a slave, as a dear brother. He is very dear to me but even dearer
to you, both as a man and as a brother in the Lord.*

*So if you consider me a partner, welcome him as you would welcome me.
If he has done you any wrong or owes you anything, charge it to me.*

PHILEMON 10-18

. . . . ● ● ● ● . . . .

THE BIBLE IS AN AMAZING BOOK. To think that an entire chapter of God's Word is devoted to an obscure runaway slave and his estranged master reflects the fact that it speaks its invincible truth to all people, regardless of their status. It also reflects the spread of the gospel throughout a world that was filled with social and moral dilemmas.

Onesimus was a slave who belonged to Philemon, a personal friend of the apostle Paul. Philemon was probably a wealthy member of the church in Colosse, which is located in what we now know as Turkey. In those days slavery was part and parcel of the Roman empire. And slaves certainly were viewed as nobodies by many Roman masters. It was so common that according to some estimates, ten thousand wealthy citizens in Rome owned nearly one million slaves. Unfortunately, many of those slaves were treated brutally, and they often sank to the lowest barbarism. The Roman society was segmented into classes—men and women, slave and free, Jews and Gentiles—and the barriers were not to be crossed.

We are not told why Onesimus fled from Philemon's house. Perhaps he resented all the sudden changes that Christianity had brought to Philemon's life and home—the prayers, the constant advice, and regulations. The text suggests that he wronged his master in some way, possibly stealing something, which he could not have done unless he had earned the trust of his master to some extent (v. 18).

Sometimes people, even today, think that if they skip the state and hide out somewhere far away, they are less likely to be discovered by the legal authorities. Onesimus evidently had the same thought, for he traveled over 1,000 miles and sought refuge in Rome, the wealthiest, most luxurious, and profligate city of the world. He probably went to hide in the Jewish quarter in Rome, which were the back slums of the city. There he would not be known or heard of anymore, so he thought, and he could live the free and easy life of a thief.

Yet the Lord looked down from heaven and set His eye of love on Onesimus. You might wonder why, with all the faithful servants He had to choose from, God chose to single out a fugitive slave who probably had embezzled some of his master's money. Weren't there better candidates among the moral and excellent of the world that infinite love should have to fix itself upon this degraded slave, who was now mixed up with the very riffraff of Roman society? But remember, " 'For my thoughts are not your thoughts, neither are your ways my ways,' declares the LORD" (Isaiah 55:8). Eternal love, which passed by kings and princes, and left Pharisees and Sadducees, philosophers and magi, to stumble in the dark as they chose, fixed its eye upon this poor runaway slave that he might come to know and serve the real Master.

The apostle Paul was imprisoned in Rome at the time and was living under house arrest, guarded in shifts by soldiers of the Praetorium. Day after day, he sat with a soldier chained to his hand, preaching to all who were admitted to hear him. His message was simple but powerful in a society where equality only existed for a certain class of people. Paul spoke of the new freedom in Christ, saying, "Here there is no Greek or Jew, circumcised or uncircumcised, barbarian, Scythian, slave or free, but Christ is all, and is in all" (Colossians 3:11).

It's not clear why Onesimus had come to Paul. Perhaps he went to see Paul, his master's friend, to beg for some help for his predicament. Running away as a slave carried a severe punishment in those days, oftentimes death. Perhaps he had reason to fear that he was about to be apprehended by authorities. Or perhaps his situation in Rome was far more uncertain than he'd imagined. The old adage, "It's greener on the other side," wasn't the case for Onesimus. Regardless of what brought Onesimus there, Paul seized the opportunity and preached Jesus to him. There was absolutely nothing spectacular about the place. To Paul, none of that mattered in the least. It wasn't a huge church, a magnificent cathedral, or a massive stadium packed with people to hear a well-known evangelist. God doesn't need awe-inspiring buildings. All He needs is a contrite and broken heart open to His stirrings. Onesimus's heart was ready to listen.

By God's providence, it was in that humble place that divine grace reached into the heart of this wild young man who had run away. And what a change it made in him immediately! Onesimus was deeply grieved as he thought about the good man he had wronged. He was deeply troubled to see the depravity of his heart as well as the error of his life, and he repented of his sin. As Paul preached Christ crucified for even a runaway slave, a load of guilt and sin lifted from Onesimus's heavy heart.

The reality of God's grace was obvious in the *character that it worked* in Onesimus after his conversion. It appears that from that very moment he must have been extremely helpful and useful because Paul was willing to have him as an associate. Onesimus was evidently of a kind, tender, and loving spirit. Paul at once called him brother and would have liked to keep him there in Rome. Onesimus, a runaway slave among millions, who by most of the Romans would be considered a worthless nobody to serve their master's needs, met a different Master and rose up to serve Him as well as His servant, the apostle Paul.

Onesimus's changed heart moved him to make restitution for the wrong he had done to Philemon, his master. He took Paul's wise advice and traveled all the way back across the Roman empire to face his master with a letter of apology in hand that was written by Paul, including a very personal IOU. Though Onesimus might have preferred to stay and serve Paul, his first duty as a new believer was to make things right with the man he had injured. Called "a son" by Paul, Onesimus is reintroduced to Philemon as more than a runaway slave come home. The change in Onesimus is a testimony to what the grace of God can do in any person! Look at the difference between the man who robbed, and the man who now comes back with a humble heart to serve his master. He is not just a repentant slave. He now is a dear brother in the faith.

LIFE LESSON

Follow Paul's example and demonstrate the same large-hearted spirit he had. Show compassion to all of God's people, especially new converts, if you find them in trouble through past wrongdoing. Do not regard them with suspicion or deal with them severely. Treat them with the love of Christ, for they are new creatures in Him (2 Corinthians 5:17). Try to help them take responsibility for their pasts and to deal appropriately with sins they may have committed toward people. Give them a brand-new start in the world. If God has forgiven them, surely we may. And if Jesus Christ has received them, let us receive them as our brothers and sisters.

CHARLES SPURGEON

PRISCILLA
and AQUILA

The Nobodies Who Dared to Speak Up

There he met a Jew named Aquila, a native of Pontus,
who had recently come from Italy with his wife Priscilla,
because Claudius had ordered all the Jews to leave Rome.
Paul went to see them, and because he was a tentmaker as they were,
he stayed and worked with them. Every Sabbath he reasoned
in the synagogue, trying to persuade Jews and Greeks. . . .

Paul stayed on in Corinth for some time. Then he left the brothers
and sailed for Syria, accompanied by Priscilla and Aquila. Before he
sailed, he had his hair cut off at Cenchrea because of a vow he had
taken. They arrived at Ephesus, where Paul left Priscilla and Aquila.
He himself went into the synagogue and reasoned with the Jews.

ACTS 18:2-4, 18-19

· ● ● ● ·

THE CONNECTION OF CORINTH with the life of Paul and the early progress of Christianity is so intertwined that every student of the Bible should have a correct and clear understanding of the historical and cultural contexts of the circumstances.

The reasons why Paul came to Corinth (over and above the discouragement he seems to have met with in Athens when few people became believers—Acts 17) were probably twofold. In the first place, it was a large mercantile city, in immediate connection with Rome and the west of the Mediterranean, with Thessalonica and Ephesus in the Aegean, and with Antioch and Alexandria in the east. The gospel, once established in Corinth, could rapidly spread

223

everywhere. And, second, from the very nature of the city, there already were a large number of Jews established there. A religion that was first to be planted in the synagogue, and was intended to scatter its seeds over all parts of the earth, could have hardly found a more favorable soil to plant itself than among the Hebrew families living at Corinth.

The success of Paul's ministry at Corinth was no doubt helped greatly by his meeting with a friend and zealous advocate of the gospel, at whose house he lodged, and with whom he obtained employment for his livelihood—the Jew Aquila from Pontus, who probably had a large workshop in the same trade by which Paul supported himself. Aquila appears not to have had a permanent residence at Rome. It appears he moved around at different times, as his business required, in various large cities situated in the center of commerce, where he found himself equally at home. But at this time he, with many others, was forced to leave Rome against his will by a mandate of the Emperor Claudius, who found in the restless, turbulent spirit of a number of Jews living in Rome (the greater part freed-men) a reason or a pretext for banishing all Jews from the city.

It is open to question whether Priscilla and Aquila were Christians when they left Rome. And seeing that Aquila is still called a Jew, the weight of authority appears that he was not a believer. It seems that while he was in Corinth that, through the preaching of Paul and the testimony of his life, Priscilla and Aquila came to embrace the tenets of Christianity. By whatever means they were led to the faith it matters little, but it is beyond dispute that, having accepted it, their lives adorned it with singular grace from that day on. Counted among Paul's helpers, while others may have been more well-known, few were more consistent or more timely with their aid as Priscilla and Aquila.

Priscilla and Aquila were tentmakers, and so Paul's association with them began at first in a purely commercial partnership. But as they lived together and worked at their trade, you can be sure they shared many earnest talks about Jesus Christ, and in the end, both husband and wife became disciples.

Often the needles of their trade would become silent as Paul told the story of Nazareth, and Calvary, and Olivet, and his own solemn experiences on the way to Damascus, until at last the tent-makers' house became a sanctuary, and all three were on their knees together in adoration of a common Lord.

Many of the earliest churches were "house churches." The believers frequently met in the house of some prominent member, and, until the fellowship grew too large for it, the meetings were held and the common meal was eaten in the large family room of a private house.

We have no record of the conversations that took place during meals over the sewing of the coarse goat's hair canvas as the three craftsmen talked together on the subjects that were nearest their hearts. But the result of it was that Aquila and his wife were both so fully equipped that they could undertake the training of others in the larger truths of the gospel.

Some time after, Paul determined to go to Ephesus. Priscilla and Aquila resolved to pack up their business and go with him. In that city they did a great work for God. Having probably a larger house than most of the early Christians, they began that "church in the house," which they seem to have continued wherever they went, for we hear of their doing the same at Rome as well (Romans 16:3).

While Priscilla and Aquila were still at Ephesus, Apollos, an eloquent preacher and "mighty in the scriptures" (Acts 18:24, KJV), arrived from Alexandria. He had, however, a serious defect in his preaching. The only Jesus he knew was an ethical Jesus, that is, Jesus as a preacher of righteousness, the Jesus of the Sermon on the Mount, Jesus as prophet, but not as priest and king. He passionately denounced sin and called on men to repent and turn to Jesus.

But when you asked what turning to Jesus meant, he was very vague and left you in the mist.

Priscilla and Aquila listened with pleasure, mingled with great pain. He was so gifted, so earnest, but as long as he preached mere morality, they felt he would do little good. But how could they help him see who Jesus really was? It was a delicate matter to tell a gifted preacher, fresh, perhaps, from the university of Alexandria, that his preaching was radically defective. Yet they had to do it. So one night we may imagine Priscilla and Aquila inviting him to their house after the sermon, and, when supper was over, beginning the delicate task. The Scriptures say Apollos "began to speak boldly in the synagogue. When Priscilla and Aquila heard him, they invited him to their home and explained to him the way of God more adequately" (Acts 18:26). Fed as they were on Paul's "strong meat," we have little doubt as to what that instruction would be. It would begin with the atonement through the blood of Christ. It would go on to salvation through faith in that blood. And it would close with the fruits of holy living, due to the presence of Christ in the believer, through the baptism of the Holy Spirit.

As they dwelt with glowing hearts on these precious truths, Apollos forgot to be offended. His candid mind received the truth as a little child, and he who before knew only the baptism of John now knew the baptism of the Holy Spirit. Apollos was a very learned man, and he could have said, "Who are these nobodies? What can simple tentmakers teach me?" But his quest for truth was paved by humility and the innocence of a child, for Jesus said, "I tell you the truth, unless you change and become like little children, you will never enter the kingdom of heaven. Therefore, whoever humbles himself like this child is the greatest in the kingdom of heaven" (Matthew 18:3-4).

It does not appear that after their stay in Ephesus, Priscilla and Aquila were closely associated with Paul, and certainly they were not among what we may call his evangelistic staff. Nor do they appear to have met him again after that time. Their gypsy life was probably forced on them by the demands of Aquila's trade. When he had made tents in Ephesus for a while, he moved on somewhere else, looking for work. Yet Paul continued to call them his "fellow workers in Christ Jesus." No matter whether it was in Corinth or in Ephesus or in Rome, these two carried Jesus Christ with them where they went, and while they were plying their trade, they also were preaching Christ.

After this we meet with the two evangelists on two other occasions, both probably at Ephesus. The first occurs in the sixteenth chapter of the Epistle to the Romans. There we read, "Greet Priscilla and Aquila, my fellow workers in Christ Jesus. They risked their lives for me. Not only I but all the churches of the Gentiles are grateful to them" (Romans 16:3-4). The text indicates they had risked their lives to save the apostle's life—when and in what circumstances we do not know. Possibly it was during the riot at Ephesus. We see that they had the true ring of Christ's heroes, the genuine martyr spirit. They were ready to take up the cross. At the same time they showed the spirit of loyal friendship.

The last reference to Priscilla and Aquila is when Paul has finished the race and in a salutatory farewell says, "Greet Priscilla and Aquila" (2 Timothy 4:19). Paul recognized his friends' love and was in debt to their enduring faithfulness. Paul's Master is not less mindful of the same quality in us who believe. "Whoever acknowledges me before men, I will also acknowledge him before my Father in heaven" (Matthew 10:32). Priscilla and Aquila were noble disciples whose lives were filled with the fruit of holy boldness to proclaim Jesus as Lord.

LIFE LESSON

· · · · · · · · · · · · · · · · • ● • · · · · · · · · · · · · · · · · ·

Faithfulness until "the race is run" is God's standard for human life—even if it means trials, tribulations, or even death. In a society where values gyrate on convenience and expediency, His eternal standard does not change. We come to see that the thing of value is not speed but endurance. The real hero is not the person who makes the fastest schedule but the one who can persevere to the end. The thing of value is not achievement but fidelity—faithfulness to follow after Him in all things as Priscilla and Aquila did so long ago.

JAMES HASTINGS

QUEEN of SHEBA

The Nobody Who Was Wowed by Solomon

*When the queen of Sheba heard about the fame of Solomon
and his relation to the name of the LORD, she came to test him with
hard questions. Arriving at Jerusalem with a very great caravan—
with camels carrying spices, large quantities of gold, and precious
stones—she came to Solomon and talked with him about all that
she had on her mind. Solomon answered all her questions;
nothing was too hard for the king to explain to her.
When the queen of Sheba saw all the wisdom of Solomon
and the palace he had built . . . she was overwhelmed.*

*She said to the king, "The report I heard in my own country
about your achievements and your wisdom is true. But I did not
believe these things until I came and saw with my own eyes. Indeed,
not even half was told me; in wisdom and wealth you have far
exceeded the report I heard. How happy your men must be! How
happy your officials, who continually stand before you and hear your
wisdom! Praise be to the LORD your God, who has delighted in you
and placed you on the throne of Israel."*

1 KINGS 10:1-9

. . . . ● ● ● ● ● . . . .

A S I SEE HER, the queen of Sheba set out on her journey to
Jerusalem with very strong and lofty motives. And she saw
and heard and took home in her heart far more than her
highest expectations. While her appearance is very brief on the
biblical stage, it is our Lord Jesus' acknowledgment and confession
of her in the coming judgment that causes her to rise out of the
throngs of visitors to Jerusalem to become singled out as one who
was amazed at Solomon's wisdom. It is this that lifts her up in my

eyes till I see her among the foremost of those who shall come from the east, and the west, and the north, and the south, who shall hear the wisdom, and taste the grace, and share the glory of the One who is far greater than Solomon in the Jerusalem that is above (Luke 11:31).

We are first told that she had heard of Solomon's fame and relationship to the name of the Lord. The name of the Lord so defines and so glorifies the whole of the Old Testament. His name is written all over Moses and David and Isaiah in letters of gold, a finger deep. In the name of the Lord is mercy, grace, patience, abundant goodness and truth, and forgiveness of sins.

No doubt this news came her way via the mercantile trade that flourished in southwest Arabia between India and east Africa and Damascus and Gaza. She recognized a connection between the wisdom of Solomon and the God whom he served. The queen of Sheba had gods of the sea and gods of the land, gods of war and gods of wine, gods of the night and gods of the day, and many more. But there was no name of any god given in Sheba that took such a hold of her heart as the name of the God of Israel.

When she came to Solomon, she asked him all the questions she had in her mind. These probably concerned matters connected with the throne and state of Sheba. Affairs of state, as we would say; her anxieties about her treaties of war and peace; her seat of judgment and justice over her own people; royal family matters also, no doubt; and matters, perhaps, still nearer her heart. Solomon's answers were of such great help that she was staggered by his wisdom.

It is thought that, among other great matters, Solomon explained to her the spiritual rationale behind the temple and all its elaborate offices and services. Now, the temple was in reality a type and prophecy of the Lord's Supper. To a woman of strong understanding and a deep heart, Solomon enlightened her about all the parts of the temple and its sacrifices to her satisfaction: the reason of this and of that; the use of this and that; the antitype of this and the antitype of that. Till, when he had taken her through it all, she was overwhelmed in spirit. *I can believe it*, she must have thought. For to this day nothing more completely subdues the spirit than when the hard questions of the heart are honestly stated and fully met and answered by the Lord. Nothing satisfies and silences the heart as does the revelation of the truth and grace of God to the person who is hungry both for His truth as it is in Jesus, and for His grace as it is in Jesus alone.

The sincerity of her appreciation and admiration for all that God had given captured the honor that both the Old Testament and our Lord bestow upon her.

LIFE LESSON

A s did the queen of Sheba, allow the Lord Jesus to take you all the more and all the deeper into His temple and show you the riches of His grace (Ephesians 1:7). Bring your questions, all your honest questions, and open your heart before Him. Hold nothing back from Him. Happy is the servant who hears His wisdom and has his heart satisfied with the all-sufficient work of Christ on the cross.

ALEXANDER WHYTE

RAHAB

The Nobody Who Made Red Her Favorite Color

*By faith the prostitute Rahab, because she welcomed the spies,
was not killed with those who were disobedient.*

HEBREWS 11:31

*In the same way, was not even Rahab the prostitute considered
righteous for what she did when she gave lodging to the spies
and sent them off in a different direction?*

JAMES 2:25

. . . . ● ● ● ● ● . . . .

I**T IS STRIKING THAT AMONG ALL** the prominent names of
the great heroes listed in the eleventh chapter of Hebrews,
men and women who by faith are said to have performed
amazing wonders, we find Rahab, the harlot of Jericho (Joshua 2:1-
7). Even more remarkable, considering the fact that she was a
Gentile known for her sinful lifestyle, Rahab's name is highlighted
among the royal genealogy of Jesus Christ (Matthew 1:5).

The apostle James also singled out Rahab. His mention of her
is remarkable because the only other person he talks about is
Abraham: Abraham the father of the Faithful, the friend of God, a
perfect and an upright man. Possibly Rahab was chosen to repre-
sent the Gentiles, in connection with the founder of Israel, who
fitly stood for the Jews. While Abraham possessed a faith that man-
ifested itself by works, so did Rahab, descended from a race
doomed to destruction, a nobody Gentile of the Gentiles. Just as
Abraham renounced his own kindred at the call of God and came
forth from Ur of the Chaldees (Genesis 12:1-5), separated unto the
Most High, Rahab left all her associations with Jericho, practically
renouncing her nationality, forsaking her country, and leaving it to

its destiny and doom, while she took her part with Israel to be a partaker with the people of God in the promised inheritance. It is no small honor for Rahab to be listed as one of the two people mentioned whose works result from faith.

Rahab demonstrated a character that deserves our attention. First of all, she possessed *remarkable faith* when you consider her circumstances. Rahab did not become a worshiper of Jehovah because her family had done so. Her parents were idolatrous Canaanites. They had no faith in God themselves, so they had none to pass on to her. It is a marvel of God's grace when we see a person of faith rising out of a family in which no true religion had ever been seen before.

Rahab's faith was also remarkable because she was *not living in a believing country.* In the whole city of Jericho, so far as we know, she was the only believer in Jehovah. If there had been other believers in the city, there would have been means found for their preservation. Jericho was neighbor to Sodom, not only as to locality but as to its idolatrous and depraved condition. When reclaimed by sovereign grace, Rahab must have found herself as much alone in Jericho as Lot had found himself alone in Sodom.

Rahab's faith was exceptional because *her access to the knowledge of Jehovah was limited.* She had no inspired book of God to read. No Jonah had gone through the streets of her city, warning the people to repent of their sins. What information she had obtained about this God of Israel, she had gathered by bits and pieces. Perhaps it was through the talk of the marketplace, the chat at the well, and the gossip outside the city gates. She had learned that a nation had come out of Egypt, and by their God, Jehovah, the Egyptian king had been destroyed at the Red Sea. Sihon, king of the Amorites, and Og, king of Bashan, had also been overthrown in battle by this people's God.

The fear of the advancing Israelites had spread over all the land, and Rahab recognized that a living God was with this people who seemed certain to conquer all of Palestine. She said within herself, "Truly, there is only one God," and her conscience responded to that declaration of faith. She believed in Jehovah the God of Israel, and she began to worship Him.

Perhaps the most amazing aspect about her faith was that she should be a woman of *such a character.* When you think about it, Rahab was an unlikely person to become a believer in Jehovah. She was a well-known harlot in all of Jericho. Yet even before the spies came, the grace of God had lifted her up out of her former life. Though her old name stuck to her, there is reason to believe that her old character was gone, and she had become a new person through the power of faith.

Her faith was *active.* When she saw the servants of God who had come as two spies, she knew at once what to do. She took them home and did her best to hide them, putting her own life at risk. She also demanded an oath from these spies that they would preserve her when the Israelites took the city. They gave her a token, a scarlet line, which she was to hang out from her window. When the time came, she put it there, because she had been told to do so.

And last, *her faith was a saving faith.* She did not bargain for just her own safety. She thought of her father, and her mother, and her brothers, and her sisters. She could not save them unless she got them under the scarlet line. Somehow, such was the influence God gave her, such was the power of her faith, that she and all her household were saved when Jericho was utterly destroyed.

From paganism to saving faith in Jehovah, Rahab went from harlot obscurity to marry Salmon, a prince of Judah, whose son, Boaz, was the great-grandfather of King David (Ruth 4:21; 1 Chronicles 2:11-12). Her place in the genealogical line of the Messiah demonstrates God's marvelous power to transform lives by His love and mercy and give them purpose and meaning in His redemptive plan for this world.

LIFE LESSON

The amazing wonder of saving grace is that it knows no boundaries. God's love can bring light to the worst of sinners in the worst of places. As you trust by faith in the precious atoning blood of Jesus Christ, He will bring you out of your horrible midnight hour and give you strength to rise out of the inky waters of sin. And as the prophet Isaiah says, "Though your sins are like scarlet, they shall be as white as snow; though they are red as crimson, they shall be like wool" (Isaiah 1:18). In Jesus, God has provided us with a scarlet line of salvation that can save us from all sin. By faith, lay hold of that scarlet line and begin a new life in Him.

CHARLES SPURGEON

THE ROMAN CENTURION

The Nobody Who Wowed Jesus

And when Jesus was entered into Capernaum, there came unto him
a centurion, beseeching him, and saying, Lord, my servant lieth at
home sick of the palsy, grievously tormented. And Jesus saith unto
him, I will come and heal him. The centurion answered and said,
Lord, I am not worthy that thou shouldest come under my roof: but
speak the word only, and my servant shall be healed. For I am a man
under authority, having soldiers under me: and I say to this man,
Go, and he goeth; and to another, Come, and he cometh;
and to my servant, Do this, and he doeth it. When Jesus heard it,
he marvelled, and said to them that followed, Verily I say unto you,
I have not found so great faith, no, not in Israel.

MATTHEW 8:5-10, KJV

. . . . ● ● ● . . . .

CENTURIONS IN THE ROMAN EMPIRE were officers chosen because of their courage and ability to lead men. They were the backbone of strength for maintaining control over the lands they had conquered. But this centurion who came to Jesus on behalf of his servant brought a different quality about him that caused Jesus Christ to marvel. When Jesus stops and marvels, we need to take notice.

From the human point of view, he was a worthy man. In fact, he was so excellent a man that even the elders of the Jews, who were by no means partial to Roman soldiers, pleaded with Jesus that he deserved to have Jesus go and heal his servant. Yet this centurion called himself unworthy when he turned toward the Lord.

237

The worthiest men in the world do not think themselves worthy, while the most unworthy people are generally those who boast of their own worthiness, and, possibly, of their own perfection.

We would not have wondered if this man had been proud, for he was one of the conquering race, and the representative of a tyrannical power known throughout the ancient world. He might even have been proud of his popularity among the Jews because he had built them a synagogue (Luke 7:4). That was a good thing to do, but it is very possible to build a synagogue, and to become a great man in one's own opinion, and stand several courses of bricks higher in pride. Few can bear to be surrounded with an atmosphere of esteem without beginning to esteem themselves much too highly. That was not the case with this centurion. He did not presume upon the greatness of his own generosity. He never even mentioned it in his request to Jesus, though others had.

He was also a man accustomed to the hierarchy of command. He only had to say to this man, "Go, and he goes." And to another, "Come," and he comes. Those who like to be obeyed are often prone to hold themselves in high esteem, but this centurion had not fallen into that common fault. He was honestly concerned about the sickness of his young servant and earnestly wanted to see him healed. He was a tender master as well as a generous neighbor. If we wished to pick out a truly worthy man, we would find him in this Roman soldier.

He was fearful of troubling the Lord with his concern. He felt that to bring Jesus through the street to his door was more than he could think of for a moment, when a word from Jesus would be sufficient to work the miracle he sought. The centurion's request is the marvelous blending of this beautiful humbleness with an extraordinary degree of faith. In his confession of humility he is unsparing, "Lord, I am not worthy that thou shouldest come under my roof" (v. 8). But in his confession of faith, he is equally clear,

"Speak the word only, and my servant shall be healed" (v. 8). Low thoughts of self should always be associated with high thoughts of Christ, for they are both products of the Spirit of God, and they help each other. Our unworthiness is but a contrast to the brightness of our Lord's infinite grace. We sink deep in humility but soar high in assurance. As we decrease, Christ increases.

This man, because he was not worthy, did not ask Christ for any mystic words or imposing ceremonies, or even so much as a visit to his house. No, he was content that the Lord should simply speak the word. This centurion, through his humility, did not have the conceit to question and doubt. His lowly estimate of himself prevented him from dictating to Jesus how the blessing should come. And because of his humility and faith, the centurion received two blessings that day: His servant was healed, and Jesus commended him for having a faith so great that He had not seen even in Israel.

LIFE LESSON

· · · · · · · · · · · · · · · · ● ● ● · · · · · · · · · · · · · · · ·

Faith and humility such as the centurion's are marvelous to Jesus Christ. Remember: "God opposes the proud but gives grace to the humble" (1 Peter 5:5). A sense of unworthiness is exceedingly useful because it puts us in a position of humility where God can bless us. We must recognize that we are undeserving and unworthy, while He is holy and glorious. When we mix humility with faith, then we will be willing to say, "Lord save me in Your own way. Your Word is enough for me." Are you content to believe God's bare Word and to be saved by God's Word alone?

CHARLES SPURGEON

SHAMGAR

The Nobody Who Really Knew How to Swing

*After Ehud came Shamgar son of Anath, who struck down
six hundred Philistines with an oxgoad. He too saved Israel. . . .*

*In the days of Shamgar son of Anath, in the days of Jael,
the roads were abandoned; travelers took to winding paths.*

JUDGES 3:31; 5:6

· ● ● ● ·

I SRAEL'S TRACK RECORD for obedience to God after the deaths
of Moses and Joshua was not very commendable. Without the
godly leadership they provided, Israel went downhill fast. For
a time they would remember Him, then they would go after the
gods of the pagan tribes around them and do evil in His sight. And
as Moses had warned their forefathers about forsaking "the Lord thy
God," divine judgment came in the form of enemies that were given
power over the Israelites. About a hundred years before the time of
Shamgar, Israel was living in a time of disobedience, and the
Scriptures say, "Once again the Israelites did evil in the eyes of the
LORD, and because they did this evil the LORD gave Eglon king of
Moab power over Israel" (Judges 3:12). But when they saw the error
of their ways and cried out to the Lord, He would send another
judge to deliver them. After Ehud's victory, there had been peace in
the land for a long time, but now Israel had abandoned the God of
their fathers again. And, once again, judgment fell on the land.

They were completely at the mercy of their old-time enemies,
the Philistines, and were desperately in need of a deliverer. Through
persistent raids their conquerors had reduced them to almost utter
want. If any Israelite succeeded in cultivating a crop of wheat, no
sooner would he have it threshed than the Philistines would swoop

down upon him like birds of prey and carry it all away. Or if any man succeeded in raising a small flock or herd, these were driven off before they were ready for the slaughter. Because of the Philistines' constant oppression, the people suffered greatly and lived in constant fear. Even their highways were growing over because the people dared not travel them for fear of being attacked (Judges 5:6).

In the wake of this calamity came an even heavier one of utter discouragement. The people of Israel saw no chance to fight back. The oppression they suffered had utterly destroyed any hope of freedom. To wake every morning fearing what the day would bring is something very few of us can comprehend in our land today. We have been blessed to live in the land of opportunities where everyone can pursue the "American Dream." But Israel at this time did not wake up to a morning filled with the bright sunshine of opportunity. They woke to a dark, bleak shadow of fear and oppression that covered their land all the time. Food shortage, raids, raping and pillaging, and even death were but minutes away any day.

Their conquerors had made sure that they would remain completely at their mercy. To prevent any fighting in self-defense, they had forced the Israelites to give up all their weapons of war. The Philistines had taken the further precaution of not allowing a single blacksmith to remain in Israel. God's chosen people were not only without weapons, but they were without any chance of making any. It is no wonder that the morale of the entire nation was broken. They were not only defeated, but they were hopeless in their defeat. They had no expectation of a better day.

Worst of all, they had lost faith in God and done evil in His sight again. The truth of the matter is that their disloyalty to Him was the very source of all their trouble. Those times of peace since Ehud's victory years ago were only faded memories now. It would be hard, therefore, to imagine a people in more desperate conditions than the people of Israel when Shamgar came upon the scene.

But even to these utterly defeated people deliverance came. You can just about imagine the surprise they had, for their deliverer came from a source from which they least expected. The man who brought about their deliverance was not a man of position. Nor was he a man with any royal blood coursing through his veins. He was not, so far as we know, even an educated man. Doubtless he had never had one single day of military training to aid him. He was a man of the people. He was a farmer—an ordinary man who was simply trying to eke out a living off the ravaged land. His greatest achievement thus far had been the breaking and driving of a yoke of oxen. Yet it was this nobody ox driver that God chose to work deliverance in Israel.

Why did God choose him? He did not choose him because he was a man obscurely placed. He did not choose him because of his disadvantages. Nor did he choose him because he was a special favorite of heaven. He chose him because Shamgar possessed certain qualities that made it possible for God to use him to bring deliverance to Israel.

Shamgar was possessed of a *noble discontent*. Now much of our discontent is far from noble, and oftentimes is quite ignoble. In fact, if we were downright honest about it, much of our present-day discontent is petty and unworthy. Sometimes it is born of an effort on our part to keep up socially in some way with our neighbors. Our little house was just fine until our neighbor built a more pretentious house. We were quite satisfied with our old Ford Country Squire station wagon until he bought a sleek black Mitsubishi Eclipse Spyder two-door convertible with leather seats. Isn't it amazing how petty discontent can make us feel disgruntled and disgusted with that which in other days had been quite satisfactory?

But there is no pettiness in the type of discontent that Shamgar was experiencing. Quite the contrary! The daily yoke of oppression made his soul sick inside that he was so cowed down and whipped and humiliated. It filled him with inner rage to see his people enslaved that way. When he saw the wheat of his neighbor carried off, when he saw his own cattle driven away to become the food of his enemies, he could not stand back and take it complacently anymore. He no longer could take it as an inevitable calamity that must be tolerated day after day, year after year. The oppressive sight made him clinch his fists every time a new raid happened. And slowly it filled his soul with fury and hot rebellion.

Now because Shamgar was filled with a burning discontent against the "status quo," there was hope for him. He was a million miles ahead of the man who had slipped into a mind-numbing cowardly contentment. It is bad to be whipped, but to be content to remain so is infinitely worse. It is bad to be in the prison house of your foes, but to lodge there till you no longer care for freedom is an even greater travesty. To be in the far country among the swine like the prodigal son is a terrible calamity. But to come to the place where you are content to live there, where you feel at home among the stench and the filth of it all, that is the very climax of calamity. To be in the Church and yet count for nothing is extremely pathetic. To be a spiritual pygmy, a moral dwarf, that is tragic indeed. But to come to the place where you persuade yourself that that is God's best for you, that is the supreme tragedy. To be content with the worst when you might have the best.

Shamgar was a man of *faith*. Every day of his life he saw the difficulties they faced as a nation as well as the rest of the men among whom he lived. He realized the strength of the Philistines as well as they. He also knew all too well the weakness of his countrymen. He understood that there were no weapons with which to fight. He himself had doubtless never seen a sword except when it had flashed in the hands of a Philistine. But the difficulties were not all that Shamgar saw. He saw the forces that make for conquest. He knew something of the history of his people. He knew how God had performed wonders for their deliverance from the bondage of Egypt. In fact, the Canaanites had feared when they heard of how Israel's God had delivered them.

Shamgar knew their history of how God had come upon the scene again and again to save them from their distress. He had heard the stories of the deliverers that God had raised up. And in this awful and trying time, there is no doubt that Shamgar turned with strong faith toward the God of his fathers. He recognized that many of the deliverances that God had wrought for Israel had been accomplished through human instrumentality. He believed in the willingness of God to use men. He even went further than that. He believed in God's willingness to use himself. It does not take a great faith for me to say, "I believe God uses men." But it does take a great faith for me to say, "I believe that God will use me." It is with this vital faith that Shamgar set about his task.

Shamgar dared to make a *beginning*. He ventured to fight when the enemy came upon him, using the weapon that he had in his hand. It was an oxgoad, probably eight to ten feet long. At one end was an iron spear, and at the other another piece of flattened metal. He had the courage to fight back regardless of the overwhelming odds that were against him. I can imagine him saying to himself, "Right here and right now I am going to stake my all on an effort to win deliverance from my enemies. They may rob me and kill me. There is every chance that they will. But that is what would likely happen if I refuse to fight. So I'm going to fight."

And that is exactly what he did, in spite of the fact that he had every reasonable excuse to sit back and do nothing. When the enemy came upon him in the field, instead of running this time, Shamgar stood his ground, armed with a seed of faith in a God who delivers His people from oppression. He knew he might not live to see another day, but those who would come to look for him would know that at least he had not died as a coward. He purposed to die fighting. So instead of waiting for a better weapon, and instead of saying what he would do if he were more fully equipped, he used what was in his hand.

And the outcome was amazing. The Scriptures say Shamgar "struck down six hundred Philistines with an oxgoad. He too saved Israel" (Judges 3:31). Shamgar won the fight that day against insurmountable odds. The man who throws himself with what he has on the side of God always wins. When the lad brings his five loaves and two fish and turns them over to Jesus, he has done his part. If Christ does not feed the multitude, then it is His own fault and not the lad's. If Shamgar strikes with his might with the weapon that God has given him, and then goes down in defeat, nobody can blame Shamgar. If you put yourself, your talents, your abilities in God's hands right now and trust Him, you will be amazed at the outcome. All God needs, all God requires for the winning of the battle in your life, is for you to place yourself in His hands and trust Him.

Shamgar not only won deliverance for himself, but he also won deliverance for his people that day. He was blessed, and he became a blessing. He seems an unlikely instrument for God to use in such a mighty fashion. His battered oxgoad seems a poor weapon for Shamgar to use. But it is not so much the instrument that counts. It is the hand that wields it, and the heart that backs the hand with a trust in God.

LIFE LESSON

· · · · · · · · · · · · · · · · · · ● ○ ● · · · · · · · · · · · · · · · · · ·

What does God's call on your life mean to you at this moment? It is not to wait for an easier time or for an easier place to be a Christian. That time and that place will never come. Your one duty is to begin in the here and now to face your foes with the weapon you have in your hands. If you will but make a beginning, you will put yourself in touch with the might of our infinite Lord. And do not despise yourself, for God loves to use what the world considers unworthy. The apostle Paul gave encouraging words inspired by the Holy Spirit when he said, "But God chose the foolish things of the world to shame the wise; God chose the weak things of the world to shame the strong. He chose the lowly things of this world and the despised things—and the things that are not—to nullify the things that are, so that no one may boast before him" (1 Corinthians 1:27-29). If you will dare today to put yourself in the hands of Jesus Christ, He will work a mighty deliverance for you personally.

GLOVIS G. CHAPPELL

THE SHUNAMMITE WOMAN

The Nobody Whose Door Was Always Open

*One day Elisha went to Shunem. And a well-to-do woman was there,
who urged him to stay for a meal. So whenever he came by,
he stopped there to eat. She said to her husband, "I know that
this man who often comes our way is a holy man of God. Let's make
a small room on the roof and put in it a bed and a table, a chair and
a lamp for him. Then he can stay there whenever he comes to us."*

2 KINGS 4:8-10

. . . . ● ● ● ● ● ● . . . .

SHUNEM WAS A LITTLE AGRICULTURAL TOWN that lay about halfway between Abel-Meholah on the Jordan, the birthplace of Elisha, and Mount Carmel, the holy place where he spent much of his time. In Shunem, there was a wealthy woman who was known by everyone to be a person of distinction. She was one of those amazing women who are never so happy as when they are doing kind acts for those around her. And her motherly concern was amplified by the fact that she had no son—that brightest joy of a Hebrew woman's heart was denied to her.

When the prophet Elisha passed through her city on his journeys to and from Mount Carmel, the Shunammite woman was pleased to take him into her home as a guest. After observing his ways and his spirit, she determined to build a room for the prophet and furnish it with simple furniture that he could use whenever he came through the area. While not extravagant, it was an extremely kind service to help make the tasks of a man of God a little easier.

If you continue to read the account in 2 Kings 4, you find that

Elisha deeply appreciated this exquisite tribute of devotion, and all the more because she made no demand upon him and expected nothing in return. Hers was an act of grace that leaves an unintended yet substantial debt on the side of the beneficiary, which the prophet was the first to feel. But even when he asked her directly as to how he might benefit her, even to the extent of mentioning her to the king, she declined his offer with a beautiful dignity.

This did not satisfy Elisha, however, and he pursued the matter until he discovered that the kindly woman had no son. Without hesitation, it seems, Elisha again called the Shunammite woman and uttered a promise that must have pierced her heart: "About this time next year, you will hold a son in your arms" (2 Kings 4:16). Surely, it seemed too good to be true, and she objected, "No, my lord. Don't mislead your servant, O man of God!" But he did not retract his word, and as the months passed, she found that the promise of the Lord would be fulfilled.

The narrative then passes over the next twelve years in silence, but you can imagine the passionate and eager delight that the Shunammite woman gave to her late-born child. For twelve years every development of his body, every new word, and every new action took immediate possession of her until the life of the mother was bound up in the life of the boy: for him to die is death for her. No, death for her is a tolerable and welcome blow in comparison to the death of her heart. And therefore no words can tell what she felt when the sudden blow fell upon her. Her boy, her one delight, was carried back from the harvest field with apparent sunstroke and by noon had passed away in her lap (2 Kings 4:20).

Her reaction is both improbable and unexpected, for she follows not reason but instinct, an instinct that is the gift of God. With a calmness that defies any explanation except for sublime faith, she immediately sets out on a journey of thirty miles to Elisha, there and back, attended by only one servant. In all probability no one but she knew that the boy was dead as she hurried toward Mount Carmel. The impression given is that she expected the prophet to cure the child of whatever illness had struck him.

From a high watchtower upon the mountain, Elisha noticed the lady riding rapidly toward him long before she saw him. To the prophet's servant, Gehazi, the Shunammite woman showed no emotion, but when she came into the presence of Elisha, she threw herself at his feet. Elisha, immediately reading the anguish of her heart, bent his attention to find out what the trouble was.

"Did I ask you for a son, my lord?" she said. "Didn't I tell you, 'Don't raise my hopes'?" (2 Kings 4:28).

Elisha understood her meaning instantly. It was his own unsolicited suggestion that she did not expect, could hardly now desire, the fulfillment of such a dream. She had returned now to hold him to that fulfillment. In no uncertain terms she let him know that she was not going to leave until he came with her. Her eyes were fixed in passionate confidence upon the prophet's face.

Second Kings 4:32-37 records the amazing miracle that took place. The vigorous pulsing life of the man, filled with the Spirit of God, was in contact with the little lifeless body that by now was growing stiff and cold. Only Elisha could explain what took place, but surely the man was walking in the presence of an unseen power, treading the threshold of life and of death. First the body warmed, and after a time the boy came fully to life. The Giver of life had restored the life of the Shunammites' only son.

It is no wonder that she was speechless and must bow down and thank the prophet to whom she owed her treasure for a second time. How could she say what was in her heart? It was one of those silent scenes more eloquent than words, which suggest why God is to our ears speechless. Speech is not the clearest and the deepest utterance. The sublimest expressions of the soul are dumb from excess of eloquence, and musical because there is no voice or language.

LIFE LESSON

It is true that God leads the souls whom He loves through unspeakable anguish at times. He quenches the light of our eyes and takes away the desire of our hearts without warning and without explanation. But the day will come when He restores them to us. Your broken heart is never forgotten by your Father in heaven. The voice of love and power will some day call you and say: Take up your son. And in that moment the rapture of recovery will explain the mystery of loss.

ROBERT HORTON

SIMEON

The Nobody Who Got a Sneak Preview

*Now there was a man in Jerusalem called Simeon, who was righteous
and devout. He was waiting for the consolation of Israel, and the
Holy Spirit was upon him. It had been revealed to him by the Holy
Spirit that he would not die before he had seen the Lord's Christ.
Moved by the Spirit, he went into the temple courts. When the par-
ents brought in the child Jesus to do for him what the custom of the
Law required, Simeon took him in his arms and praised God, saying:
"Sovereign Lord, as you have promised, you now dismiss your ser-
vant in peace. For my eyes have seen your salvation, which you have
prepared in the sight of all people, a light for revelation to the
Gentiles and for glory to your people Israel."*

*The child's father and mother marveled at what was said about him.
Then Simeon blessed them and said to Mary, his mother, "This child
is destined to cause the falling and rising of many in Israel, and to be
a sign that will be spoken against, so that the thoughts of many
hearts will be revealed. And a sword will pierce your own soul too."*

LUKE 2:25-35

THAT SCENE, when the old man Simeon takes the infant
Jesus in his withered arms, is one of the most picturesque
and striking in all of the Gospel narratives. Simeon's whole
life appears, in its later years, to have been under the immediate
direction of the Spirit of God. Though he may have been nothing
but an old man, a nobody in the eyes of others, who hung around
the temple, he did not go unnoticed by God.

It is remarkable to notice how, in the course of three consecutive
verses, the operation of that divine Spirit in his life is mentioned, for

it says, ". . . the Holy Spirit was upon him" (v. 25). He had such a close relationship to God that he recognized the stirrings of the Holy Spirit in his soul. And the Spirit had made a remarkable promise to him that he would not die until he had seen the Lord's Christ (v. 26). And with that expectation burning within his heart every day, he was led by the Spirit to go up to the temple that day to worship in holy expectation.

Think of the old man, waiting there in the sanctuary, told by God that he was about to have the fulfillment of his lifelong desire, and yet probably not knowing what kind of a shape the fulfillment would take. There is no reason to believe that he knew he was to see an infant, and so he waits and prays, as was his custom. And presently a peasant woman comes in with a child in her arms. Suddenly there arises in his soul that unmistakable voice of the Holy Spirit he had come to know, which now told him, "Anoint Him, for this is He!" And so, whether he expected such a vision or not, he takes the Child in his arms and says, "Lord! Now, now— after all these years of waiting—You have kept Your promise to me, so let Your servant depart in peace."

It is striking to observe how the description of Simeon's character expresses the aim of the whole Old Testament revelation—to restore the image of God in His people. All that was meant by the preceding long series of manifestations through all these years was accomplished in this man. Listen to how Simeon is described: "who was righteous and devout" (v. 25); that is the perfection of moral character, stated in the terms of the Old Testament; "waiting for the consolation of Israel"; that is the ideal attitude that the entirety of the gradual manifestation of God's increasing purpose running through the ages was intended to make in the attitude of every true Israelite—an expectant, eager look forward, and in the present, the fulfilling of all duties to God and man. "And the Holy Spirit was upon him"—that description of Simeon, in a measure, was the ultimate aim of the whole revelation given to Israel. So this man stands as an embodiment of the very results that God had patiently sought through millenniums of providential dealing and inspiration. Therefore, in this man's arms was placed the Christ for whom he had been waiting so long.

Simeon also demonstrates what God had intended to obtain by all the previous revelations. He recognized that they were transcended and complete, and that they all pointed to that very moment there in the temple. He, a devout Israelite, was now staring in wonder at the Incarnate Messiah—the living culmination of all the prophecies he had treasured in his heart for years. And so he rejoices in the Christ that he receives into his arms and declares his praise and thanksgiving for having lived to see the appearing of the One who would redeem not only Israel, but the whole world.

Simeon's song of praise is also the realization that he knows his days are drawing to an end: "Sovereign Lord, as you have promised, you now dismiss your servant in peace" (v. 29). Yet he welcomes the approach of death. The actual word used conveys the idea of the hour having come to relieve a sentry from his post. He has been on the watch all through the long, weary night, or toiling through a hot, dusty day, and now may extinguish his lantern, or fling down his ax and go home to his hut. Simeon has lived to see his dream come true, and now he welcomes the approach of death with dignity. He feels no agitation, no fluster of any kind, but quietly slips away from his post. And the reason for that peaceful welcome of the end is the gift God had given him: "For my eyes have seen your salvation . . . a light for revelation to the Gentiles and for glory to your people Israel" (vv. 30-32).

That sight of the Savior is the reason, first of all, for his being sure that the curfew had rung for him, and that the day's work was done. But it is also the reason for the peacefulness of his departure. He went in peace because the weary, blurred, old eyes had seen all that any man needs to see to be satisfied and blessed. Life could yield nothing more, though its length were doubled to Simeon, than the sight of God's salvation.

LIFE LESSON

A re you facing the end of your days? Is your heart burdened or weary? Then listen to the apostle John, who writes of Jesus, "I stand at the door and knock. If anyone hears my voice and opens the door, I will come in and eat with him, and he with me" (Revelation 3:20). If you have opened the door of your heart to the Savior—be it years ago or even now at the hour of your death—then let your heart rejoice. You may go in peace, for your eyes have seen Him who satisfies our vision, whose bright presence will go with you into the darkness of death, yet whom you will see more perfectly when you open your eyes in His presence and are taken to be a son or daughter in your Father's house.

ALEXANDER MACLAREN

SIMON *of* CYRENE

The Nobody Who Got More Than He Bargained For

*A certain man from Cyrene, Simon, the father of Alexander
and Rufus, was passing by on his way in from the country,
and they forced him to carry the cross.*

MARK 15:21

*As they led him away, they seized Simon from Cyrene,
who was on his way in from the country, and put the cross
on him and made him carry it behind Jesus.*

LUKE 23:26

. . . . ● ● ● ● . . . .

L ET'S FACE IT, some men and women are naturally born to
distinction. They inherit an honored name, a name that has
been associated with dignity and power for generations. At
the right time they step into an eminent position prepared for them
and suddenly are observed by all. Whatever their characters may be,
their position renders them conspicuous. Others win distinction for
themselves. There is nothing remarkable about them to begin with.
But eventually they demonstrate that they have qualities of an
uncommon stamp. By their character of genius they *command* the
attention of others and at last rise to distinction and fame.

Yet there is another class still, though it is considerably smaller
perhaps than either of these two. It is composed of unknown people who have honors thrust upon them without any effort or even
desire on their part. They are often unwilling to accept them and
feel them a burden rather than a pleasure. Simon the Cyrenian
belonged to this last class of people. Among the throngs gathering
at Passover, he was just another nameless pilgrim, yet this day he
was forced to become a distinguished man in spite of himself.

He had traveled a long way to celebrate the Passover in Jerusalem. Cyrene was a city in North Africa, what we know today as Tripoli, the capital of Libya, at least eight hundred miles from Israel. It was a city where a colony of Jews had been established long before. And as Simon set out on a long journey to celebrate the Passover, he had no idea what awaited him. When you think of it, the timing of his arrival as he walked into Jerusalem that morning was remarkable. Little did he suspect that he would end up carrying a cross for a condemned man before the day was over. Had Simon suspected anything of the kind, he probably would have stayed at home. Cross-bearing was a path to distinction that he had no ambition to travel. And yet Simon became a famous man that day.

A brief verse from each of the Gospel writers is all the information we have about Simon. Yet each glimpse is not just the echo of the others. Each inspired writer describes the incident in his own way. And so we find, as might be expected, a unique touch supplied by one that is not given by the others. Taken all together they help to complete a picture for us of what took place that day. We see the melancholy procession of Jesus' crucifixion on its way from the Praetorium to Calvary.

Jesus is walking in the midst of soldiers. Accompanying Him are two thieves, who have been condemned to the same tragic end. The Roman soldiers are there in strong force, with their centurion at their head, charged with the safeguarding of the prisoners and the carrying out of the cruel sentence of crucifixion.

As the procession moves through street after street, people come out of their houses to inquire what it all means, and to add to Jesus' reviling foes or to His few silent friends, depending on how the sight happens to stir them. Finally, the procession reaches the gate of the city and heads for the hill in the open country beyond the walls, where ceremonial defilement from dying criminals is no longer feared.

The criminal who was to be crucified had to carry the cross from the hall of judgment to the place of execution. Jesus had begun to carry the cross according to this custom, but He now gives way beneath its weight. The terrible physical suffering He has endured from being whipped has drained all His strength away. Now He sinks to the ground exhausted and almost fainting as the cross presses Him to the earth. The soldiers are in a dilemma. It is obvious that Jesus needs help, for He cannot go any farther. Yet the soldiers will certainly not lower themselves by helping a criminal to carry His cross. Nor will the Jews do anything to assist. They would vehemently reject the idea of touching that accursed piece of wood, the symbol of the Roman despotism that they all hated. The soldiers look around for someone who will serve their purpose, but they see no one. They are almost at their wits' end. But just at that moment they catch sight of Simon of Cyrene.

Simon is on his way into the city, rejoicing as he comes near the gate at the prospect of ending a long journey, and of arriving in time to join in the Passover celebrations. He is on a pilgrimage to the Holy City, and his heart is filled with lofty and sacred feelings. He has traveled a great distance to observe the most sacred of Jewish feasts. And here is the Divine Paschal Lamb coming forth to meet him, on His way to be slain on Calvary. Could it be that Simon would see in that procession toward Golgotha the fulfillment of his grandest hopes? Jesus bending and ready to fall under His heavy cross, and going to die upon it—could this be the glory of Israel, the long-awaited Messiah? Was it true that the Paschal Lamb, associated with the great deliverance from Egypt's bondage, slain, roasted, eaten, was after all the type of the true Messiah, and that Simon, coming to observe the type, was to find in that cross-bearing Jesus on His way to Calvary the veritable antitype? We have reason to believe that that is exactly what Simon came to know and experience that day.

What moved Simon to take that particular turning that brought him to Christ and His cross just at the very moment he was needed? God's divine providence! For if he had delayed a minute or two, he would have been too late. He is like the man mentioned in our Savior's parable, who was walking home one evening across the fields, when suddenly he noticed a place where the rains had washed the earth away, and there unexpectedly found a treasure (Matthew 13:44). Simon, too, found something that day that he had never expected to find, something he had never once thought of, but ever after it was the treasure of his life.

When the centurion ordered him to help carry Jesus' cross, Simon probably felt that this encounter at that precise moment was the most unfortunate incident that could have befallen him—an interruption, an annoyance, and a humiliation. Yet it turned out to be the very gateway of life for him. Very often God wants to send us blessings, but we tend to have our own little checklist of expectations as to how they should come. Often the circumstances and the people God uses aren't what we expect. Blessings sometimes come in disguise, and we may cry out in fear at the way they appear, but then suddenly the Son of Man appears with His new resurrection life for whatever we may be facing.

Whatever form of cross-bearing is laid upon us, at first we feel the burden as trying and oppressive. We feel the pain of having to give up our own way and to have our liberty restricted. We don't like having anyone telling us what to do. We are filled with resentment against the gospel of Christ for spoiling our plans and pleasures. But as God's grace works in us and makes us willing, eventually we will come to love the service that we hated the most. The cross that crushed us to the earth will support us and lift us to heaven with a new life that far surpasses what we had known before. The compulsion of painful circumstances that brought us to Christ in the first place will issue in richer life and grander liberty, and the service forced upon us will be changed into a lifelong faithfulness.

Simon's experience might have had the opposite effect from what it did have, and in his heart he might have cursed not only the soldiers and the mob, but Christ Himself, the innocent cause of his misfortune. It is true that cross-bearing does not always bring blessing with it, or lead those who have to suffer nearer to Christ. It all depends on the condition of the person's heart. With some it tends to harden their hearts against God's pleadings with them and to make them sullen and defiant. And yet it is clearly one of God's ways—it may seem to us a very roundabout way—of stopping us when we are going down our own stubborn paths. We should pray to be able to see His hand in it, and to get out of it all the good and blessing He intends for us.

Simon came to realize that though he thought he was carrying the cross for Christ that day, Christ had really been carrying it for him. And so what he had shrunk from as a disgrace and a pain, he welcomed as an honor and a joy. By becoming a Christian, he bore his Master's cross all his life and walked by His side not only for a few minutes on the way to Calvary, but every day back in the streets of Cyrene.

Carrying the cross for Christ was an immeasurable gain to Simon. This divine encounter issued in his salvation and the salvation of his house. The Gospel of Mark calls him "the father of Alexander and Rufus" (Mark 15:21). Evidently the two sons were well-known to those for whom Mark was writing; that is, they were members of the Christian circle. And there can be little doubt that the connection of his family with the church was the result of this incident in their father's life. Mark wrote his gospel for the Christians of Rome, and in the Epistle to the Romans one Rufus is mentioned as resident there along with his mother (Romans 16:13). This may have been one of the sons of Simon. And in Acts 13:1, one Simeon—the same name as Simon—is mentioned along with a Lucius of Cyrene as a noticeable Christian at Antioch. Altogether, we have sufficiently clear indications that as a result of this encounter with Jesus that day, Simon became a Christian. It would have been contrary both to nature and to grace that any man should come so near Jesus, and should do so much for Him, and not be called into His kingdom.

But Mark tells us at the same time that Simon's reward was greater than the saving of his own soul. It was the answer of his constant and urgent prayers. Away in Cyrene, this pilgrim to the Holy City had left two little sons, and as he looked upon them, exiles from the land of Israel, as he taught them the fear of the God of Jacob, the very passion of his heart overflowed with prayer, that they might grow in the faith and obedience to God. Christ read the heart of His cross-bearer as he walked by His side. He saw the names Rufus and Alexander graven on Simon's heart. And the great reward was given to Simon of seeing both his sons known and loved and honored in the Church of Christ.

LIFE LESSON

· · · · · · · · · · · · · · · · · ● ● ● · · · · · · · · · · · · · · · · · ·

Why do you fear to take up the cross that has suddenly loomed up in front of you? You must bear it, for it leads to an eternal kingdom. In the cross is salvation, in the cross is life, in the cross is strength of mind, in the cross joy of spirit, in the cross the height of virtue, in the cross the perfection of holiness. There is no salvation of the soul, or hope of everlasting life, save in the cross. Take up, therefore, your cross and follow Jesus. For if you are dead with Him, you will also live with Him. And if you are a partaker of His sufferings, you will be a partaker also of His glory. Everything depends upon the cross, and all lies in our dying there. Death on the cross is the gateway to life! Like Simon, as you bear the cross of death, eternal life will spring up for you and influence those you carry in your heart.

JAMES HASTINGS

SUSANNA, JOANNA, and MARY

The Nobodies Who Found Mundane Jobs a Joy

After this, Jesus traveled about from one town and village to another,
proclaiming the good news of the kingdom of God. The Twelve were
with him, and also some women who had been cured of evil spirits
and diseases: Mary (called Magdalene) from whom seven demons
had come out; Joanna the wife of Cuza, the manager of Herod's
household; Susanna; and many others. These women were helping
to support them out of their own means.

LUKE 8:1-3

· ● ● ● ● ·

THE EVANGELIST LUKE has preserved for us several incidents in our Lord's life in which women play a prominent part. It is worth observing that we owe to Luke these revealing details, and the fact that the service of these grateful women lasted during the entire time of our Lord's wandering life after He left Galilee.

An incidental reference about these women is found in Matthew's account of the crucifixion (Matthew 27:55-56), but had it not been for Luke, we would not have known the names of two or three of them, nor would we have known how constantly they ministered to Him. As to the women of the little group, we know very little about them. To the religious leaders of the day, they would be considered frivolous nobodies following after a deluded man. Mary of Magadala had had a very hard life. The Scripture record of her is very sweet and beautiful. Delivered by Christ from that mysterious demoniacal possession, she devoted herself to Him, as a true woman, with all her heart.

She is one of the little group whose strong love, casting out all fear, gave the others the strength and dauntless courage to stand by the cross when all the men except the gentle apostle of love, John, as he is called, were cowering in the corners, afraid for their lives. This Mary was one of the same group who continued their faithful ministry beyond Jesus' death, for they brought sweet spices with them in order to anoint Him. And it was the same Mary whose unfaltering devotion was rewarded when she came upon the risen Lord and exclaimed, "Rabboni! (which means Teacher)" (John 20:10-18). In that one moment, all the tears of grief were instantly changed into an inexpressible joy that would never leave her.

Then as to Joanna, the wife of Cuza, Herod's steward, old Church tradition tells us that she was the spouse of the nobleman whose son Christ healed at Capernaum. But the text before us seems to indicate that she was one of the women who had received healing from the hands of Jesus: "The Twelve were with him, and also some women who had been cured of evil spirits and diseases" (v. 1). And then as for Susanna, is it not an honor to be known to all the world forever by one single line of Scripture for the service she gave to Jesus?

To understand why these women gave themselves and their means to minister to Jesus, we look at what He said about Himself, "Foxes have holes and birds of the air have nests, but the Son of Man has no place to lay his head" (Matthew 8:20). He had not a thing that He could call His own, and when He came to the end of His life there was nothing for His executioners to gamble for except His one possession, the seamless robe (John 19:23-24). He is hungry, and there is a fig tree by the roadside, and He comes, expecting to get His breakfast off that (Matthew 21:19). He is tired, and He borrows a fishing boat to lie down and sleep in (Luke 8:22-23).

He is thirsty, and He asks a woman of questionable character to give Him a drink of water (John 4:5-7). And even when he rides into Jerusalem knowing the Crucifixion is only days away, He rides on a donkey that belongs to others (Matthew 21:2).

Sometimes we forget what life must have been like back then. In our modern age, we can get anything we need 24/7 to satisfy our needs. Not so in Jesus' time. He and His disciples were busy, yet they had very practical needs as they walked around from village to village, which these women saw and determined to supply. There was food to buy and cook; firewood to find and chop for their fires; and sweaty and dusty clothes to wash at the riverside. Nothing illustrious that we might consider as meaningful service, but it was a service done out of devoted love and humility for all Jesus had done for these women.

They had a personal consciousness of redemption, for the text says, ". . .women who had been cured of evil spirits and diseases" (v. 2). They had felt the liberating touch of Jesus to their bodies and their souls, which instantly evoked from the depths of their hearts a gratitude that ached to express itself in service to the One who had blessed them. Love born out of gratitude never needs an elevated job to give self-worth. A life that has been touched by He who is Love Eternal deems the most insignificant of tasks a privilege for His sake. There is no true service in His kingdom except it be the expression of love. That is the one great Christian principle, and the other is that there is no love that does not rest on the consciousness of redemption. And from those two flow all the distinct characteristics of Christian ethics.

Jesus has told us how we can continue the service that these women counted as a privilege to offer Him. We have a whole world full of opportunities waiting at our doorstep, for Jesus Himself said, "I tell you the truth, whatever you did for one of the least of these brothers of mine, you did for me" (Matthew 25:40). We do not have to look far to find a person who needs some kind of service.

Jesus let these women help Him that He might live to bear the cross. He lets you and me help Him for that for which on the cross He died—taking His message of salvation to the whole world. These women's names will never perish as long as the world lasts. How many deeds of faithful love and noble devotion are all compressed into those words, "These women were helping to support them out of their own means" (v. 3). Our text also says "many others." Do you not think that these anonymous women who ministered to Jesus were as dear to Him as Mary and Joanna and Susanna? A great many people helped Him whose deeds are related in the Gospels, but whose names are not recorded. But what does it matter that the world does not know their names? They are all written in the Lamb's book of life. And so the work is eternal and will last on in our consciousness and in His remembrance, who will never forget any of it. And on that day of His second coming, He will judge all our deeds and with great joy reward us for the faithful service we gave when the world passed us by and did not take notice.

LIFE LESSON

There will come days in our service to God when we may question whether what we do really matters at all. The joy we first had may have slipped into a monotonous drudgery. And the present task we do for Jesus may seem a waste of time. That is exactly what the enemy of our souls wants us to think. But at those low times, we must remember what the apostle Paul exhorted: "The Lord will reward everyone for whatever good he does, whether he is slave or free" (Ephesians 6:8). No matter what we do, let us do it for the Lord, and in the end, He will put a meaning into our work and a majesty into it that we know nothing about at the present time. When we have in our poor love poorly ministered unto Him who in His great love died for us, then, at the last day, the wonderful word will be fulfilled: "It will be good for those servants whose master finds them watching when he comes. I tell you the truth, he will dress himself to serve, will have them recline at the table and will come and wait on them" (Luke 12:37).

ALEXANDER MACLAREN

THE SYROPHOENICIAN WOMAN

The Nobody Who Wasn't Ashamed to Eat Leftovers

Leaving that place, Jesus withdrew to the region of Tyre and Sidon.
A Canaanite woman from that vicinity came to him, crying out,
"Lord, Son of David, have mercy on me! My daughter is suffering
terribly from demon-possession."

Jesus did not answer a word. So his disciples came to him
and urged him, "Send her away, for she keeps crying out after us."

He answered, "I was sent only to the lost sheep of Israel."

The woman came and knelt before him. "Lord, help me!" she said.

He replied, "It is not right to take the children's bread
and toss it to their dogs."

"Yes, Lord," she said, "but even the dogs eat
the crumbs that fall from their masters' table."

Then Jesus answered, "Woman, you have great faith! Your request is
granted." And her daughter was healed from that very hour.

MATTHEW 15:21-28

. . . . ● ● ● ● . . . .

J ESUS HAD JUST FINISHED EXPLAINING a parable to His
disciples and then withdrew to the ancient Phoenician region
of Tyre and Sidon, which is northwest of Galilee. Mark's Gospel
says, "He entered a house and did not want anyone to know it; yet
he could not keep his presence secret" (Mark 7:24). It didn't take
long before His presence became known to those in the city. As soon
as this Syrophoenician woman heard that Jesus was there, she came
immediately seeking help for her daughter who was possessed by
an evil spirit.

Matthew calls this woman a Canaanite, which would clearly indicate to any Jew that she was descended from a lineage of people who were the enemies of Israel. Mark's Gospel refers to her as a Greek, born in Syrian Phoenicia (Mark 7:26). Both Gospel accounts clearly indicate that she was a Gentile, a nobody's nobody—someone whom the Jews, particularly the disciples, would prefer to avoid.

But we must remember that Jesus was about His Father's business at all times. And even His departure into that Gentile land was not without purpose. The brightest jewels are often found in the darkest places. Let us also go even to the borders of Tyre and Sidon, though the land be under a curse, for even there we shall discover some elect one, ordained to be a jewel for the Redeemer's crown. Our heavenly Father has children everywhere.

This Syrophoenician woman was a woman of amazing faith, though she could have heard but little of Him in whom she believed, and perhaps had never seen Him at all until the day when she fell at His feet and said, "Lord, help me!"

The Scriptures say that "Jesus did not answer a word" (v. 23). But she did not give up. Her child's need was very urgent, her motherly heart was very tender, and her cries were very piercing. As if He were deaf and dumb, Jesus seemed to ignore her. Yet she was not staggered. She believed in Him, and even He Himself could not make her doubt Him. Her persistence so clearly demonstrates that *the mouth of faith cannot be closed even on account of the closed ear and the closed mouth of Christ.*

Jesus had a very quick eye for spying faith. If the jewel was lying in the mire, His eye caught its glitter. Faith had a strong attraction for the Lord Jesus, and He was charmed with the fair jewel of this woman's faith. Watching and delighting in it, He resolved to turn it round and set it in other lights so that the various facets of this priceless diamond might each one flash its brilliance and delight His soul. Therefore He tried her faith by His silence and by His discouraging replies that He might see its strength. But He was all the while delighting in it and secretly sustaining it.

Even the disciples did not treat her well. But no matter what they said, she demonstrated that *her faith could not be silenced by their unkind conduct.* They were not like their Master yet, and at times they tried to prevent people from approaching Him. May we not have the insensitive hearts they displayed when needs come begging at our feet. They were too busy attending to the spiritual lessons they were learning from the Master. Yet the very reason for His coming was right in front of them, but perhaps they were blinded by prejudice.

Whatever they thought, for sure she annoyed them, for she would not stop shouting out for help. She kept pleading her case with boundless perseverance. Finally, they went to Jesus and said, "Send her away, for she keeps crying out after us" (v. 23). She never cried *after them*; it was after their Master. Cold, hard words and unkind, unsympathetic behavior could not prevent her from pleading with Him in whom she believed.

Finally Jesus spoke, but His words are not what one would expect: "I was sent only to the lost sheep of Israel" (v. 24). Despite His answer, her mouth *was not closed by exclusive doctrine, which appeared to confine the blessing to a favored few.* She came and knelt before Him and said, "Lord, help me!" (v. 25) There is a house of Israel not after the flesh but after the spirit, and therefore the Syrophoenician woman was included even when it appeared she was shut out.

Jesus replied, saying, "It is not right to take the children's bread and toss it to their dogs" (v. 26). When Christ spoke of dogs, He meant that the Gentiles were to Israel as dogs. She did not contest it but yielded by saying, "Yes, Lord." She did not raise a question or dispute the justice of the Lord's dispensing His own grace according to His sovereign good pleasure.

At this point, there is no doubt that her sense of unworthiness was very deep. She did not expect to win the answer she sought on any merit of her own. She depended entirely on the goodness of Christ's heart, not on the goodness of her cause, and upon the excellence of His power rather than on the prevalence of her plea. Yet conscious as she was that she was only a poor Gentile dog, her prayers were not hindered. *Her mouth of faith was not even closed by a sense of admitted unworthiness.*

Perhaps she did not see all that Jesus might have meant, yet her faith was not quenched. It was a faith of that immortal kind that nothing can kill. Her mind was made up that whatever Jesus meant, or did not mean, she would not cease to trust Him and would urge Him to meet her need. It was a faith that did not argue. Faith pleads but never argues. Faith in God implies agreement with what God says and consequently excludes the idea of doubt.

Despite His answer, her faith prevailed further, seen in the humility and hope in her answer: " 'Yes, Lord,' she said, 'but even the dogs eat the crumbs that fall from their masters' table' " (v. 28). Her faith has been sufficiently tried, and now Jesus brings it forth as gold and sets His own royal mark of approval on it with these memorable words, "O woman, great is your faith! Let it be to you as you desire" (Matthew 15:28, KJV). And her daughter was set free that very hour.

LIFE LESSON

· · · · · · · · · · · · · · · · • ● • · · · · · · · · · · · · · · · ·

This woman is a lesson to all who might think they are beyond hope. Take heart and comfort, and come to Jesus Christ and trust yourselves in His hands. She is an example to those who have made attempts at self-reformation and failed miserably. Trust in Him whose blood has not lost its power to cleanse from every sin, whose promise has not lost its truth, and whose arm has not lost its power to save. She is a lesson for every intercessor. When you pray for a fellow sinner, do not do it in a cold-hearted manner. Plead as for your own soul and your own life. And lastly, she is a lesson to every mother, for she was pleading for her daughter. Maternal instinct makes the weakest strong, and the most timid brave.

CHARLES SPURGEON

THE WOMAN WHO WAS *a* SINNER

The Nobody Who Crashed the Party

When a woman who had lived a sinful life in that town learned that Jesus was eating at the Pharisee's house, she brought an alabaster jar of perfume, and as she stood behind him at his feet weeping, she began to wet his feet with her tears. Then she wiped them with her hair, kissed them and poured perfume on them.

When the Pharisee who had invited him saw this, he said to himself, "If this man were a prophet, he would know who is touching him and what kind of woman she is—that she is a sinner."

LUKE 7:37-39

· ● ● ● ·

HOW DARE THIS WOMAN enter the house of Simon the Pharisee! To the "righteous" of her day, she was not just a nobody. She was an immoral woman who, in their eyes, deserved to be stoned. She knew full well that her very presence would be an offense to the man who counted himself so righteous. Yet we, like Simon, are often quick to recognize the "sinner" in others. But in the case now before us, Jesus saw something much deeper, something more precious to His heart than what Simon saw. The anointing this woman offered was that of a poor returning wanderer, who, under a deep sense of gratitude, brought the best she had to her Lord and was accepted by His grace.

Grace, the most costly of spikenard: This story literally drips with it like those Oriental trees that bleed perfume. Grace, sovereign, distinguishing, omnipotent, is exceedingly magnified in how Jesus dealt with this woman who was a sinner.

Grace is demonstrated here *in its object*. She was "a sinner"—a sinner not in the flippant, unmeaning, everyday sense of the term, but a sinner in the blacker, filthier, and more obnoxious sense. She had forsaken the guide of her youth and forgotten the covenant of her God. She had sinned against the laws of purity and had made herself a defiled vessel. She was one of the scarlet sinners that we read of in Scripture—she sinned and seduced others to sin with her, and everyone knew it.

Yet, miracle of miracles, she was an object of the distinguishing grace of Jesus! Was this an extraordinary and out-of-the-way instance of divine mercy? By no means, for the grace of God has frequently chosen the lowest of the low and the vilest of the vile. Remember how, in the genealogy of the Lord, you find the name of the shameless Tamar, the harlot Rahab, and the unfaithful Bathsheba, as if to indicate that the Savior of sinners would enter into a close relationship with the most degraded and fallen of our race. This is, in fact, one of the dearest titles of our Lord, though it was hissed at Him from the lips of contempt, "A friend of publicans and sinners." This is Jesus' character, of which He is not ashamed.

Grace has fallen upon the most unlikely cases in order to show itself to be truly grace. It has found a dwelling place for itself in the most unworthy heart so that its freeness might be seen more clearly. If your heart expresses deep sorrow over your sin—let this thought comfort you and give you hope for mercy: Some of the grossest blasphemers, persecutors, thieves, fornicators, and drunkards have been forgiven, renewed, and made to live sober, righteous, and godly lives. These have obtained mercy in them first so that God might show forth His long-suffering as a comfort and encouragement to others to cry out to Him for mercy.

This woman's reaction is that of a hardened heart touched by the love of God. When someone discovers that God has chosen them, when they feel that grace has broken their heart, has brought them to Christ, and has covered them with a perfect righteousness, they break out in wondering exclamation, "How could You, Lord, have chosen me?" The more a believer looks within, the more he discovers reasons for divine wrath, and the less he believes in his own personal merit. And yet the heart of a true believer is filled with adoring gratitude that the Lord's boundless love should have been pleased to settle and fix itself upon him!

Grace is greatly magnified in *its fruits*. Who would have ever thought that a woman who had yielded her members to be servants of unrighteousness should now become a maid of honor to the King of kings? She offered hospitalities to Jesus that Simon the Pharisee omitted, and she offered them in an infinitely better spirit and style than Simon could have done even if he had tried! She did not come to Jesus in her own righteousness, but with a "broken and contrite spirit" that David spoke of (Psalm 51:17). Earlier in this chapter, Jesus had been preaching the gospel, and more especially to the poor. Perhaps she stood in the street attracted by the crowd, and as she listened to Jesus' words, His words moved her greatly.

She had never heard a man speak after that fashion, and when He spoke of abounding mercy and the willingness of God to accept as many as would come to Him, the tears began to flow down her cheeks. And when she heard Him tell of the Father in heaven who would receive prodigals and embrace them in His loving arms, her hardened heart began to break on grace. She turned from her evil lifestyle and became a new woman, desirous of better things, anxious to be freed from sin.

But would such pardoning love reach even to her? The more she listened to Jesus' gentle words, the more her faith grew, and with it an ardent love. And so she slipped into the house of the Pharisee to pay homage to the One who had filled her heart with a hope she never dreamed possible after all she had done. When she saw that the Pharisee had refused Jesus the ordinary courtesy of washing His feet, and that they were all stained and travel-worn with His long journeys of love, she began to weep, and the tears fell in such plenteous showers that they even washed His feet. Here was holy water of a true sort. The crystal of penitence falling in drops, each one as precious as a diamond.

Grace is the great source and cause of all complete morality—indeed, there is no real holiness in the sight of God except that which grace creates, and which grace sustains. This woman, apart from grace, would have remained defiled to her dying day, but the grace of God worked a marvelous transformation, removing the impudence of her face, the flattery from her lips, and the lust from her heart. Eyes that were full of adultery were now fountains of repentance. Lips that were doors of lascivious speech, now yielded holy kisses to the Savior's feet—the profligate was a penitent, the castaway a new creature.

All the actions that are attributed to this woman illustrate the transforming power of divine grace. She wept abundantly. She wept out of no mere sentimentalism, but at the remembrance of her many crimes. As her tears spilled onto Jesus' feet, she remembered the dangerous paths into which she had wandered. Note her humility in the position she took at His feet. Those who serve the Lord Jesus truly have a holy bashfulness, a shrinking sense of their own unworthiness, and are content to fulfill the very lowest office in His household.

She was a woman of *great courage* to enter a Pharisee's house. The look of a Pharisee to this woman must have been enough to freeze summer into howling winter. How fearless she was and how bravely she held her tongue when Simon railed against her to the Lord. And yet when Simon presumed the Lord's ignorance of what kind of woman she was, we see grace in another facet of its beauty. The Lord Jesus Christ *became the defender of the penitent.*

Jesus by His parable in her defense showed that He was justified in letting the woman approach, because great love prompted her. Jesus said to the Pharisee, "Two men owed money to a certain moneylender. One owed him five hundred denarii, and the other fifty. Neither of them had the money to pay him back, so he canceled the debts of both. Now which of them will love him more?" (Luke 7:41-42) There was no sin in her approach, but much to commend, since her motive was pure and excellent. The motive is the true measure of a deed. She felt intense love and gratitude toward the person who had forgiven her. And to the amazement of all, He justified her in front of the very one who would condemn her.

Jesus turned toward the woman and said to the Pharisee, "Do you see this woman? I came into your house. You did not give me any water for my feet, but she wet my feet with her tears and wiped them with her hair. You did not give me a kiss, but this woman, from the time I entered, has not stopped kissing my feet. You did not put oil on my head, but she has poured perfume on my feet. Therefore, I tell you, her many sins have been forgiven—for she loved much. But he who has been forgiven little loves little" (v. 44-47).

Jesus in all tenderness turned to her and said, "Your sins are forgiven." What riches of grace! From that moment full assurance of faith must have filled her soul. And she departed with yet another of His gifts of grace: "Your faith has saved you; go in peace."

LIFE LESSON

· · · · · · · · · · · · · · · · ● ● ● ● ● · · · · · · · · · · · · · · · ·

To what extent have you experienced what grace can do for you? If He has lifted you up out of the miry clay of sin, He can do more. He can set your feet upon a rock. He can put a new song into your mouth and establish you in righteousness. You do not know the exceeding bounty of your own heavenly Father. Unfathomable is His goodness. Arise and enjoy it. Then go out and share His grace with all who need to be lifted out of their own pits of sin, for "through Christ Jesus the law of the Spirit of life set me free from the law of sin and death" (Romans 8:2).

CHARLES SPURGEON

THE WOMAN WITH *the* ISSUE *of* BLOOD

The Nobody Who Couldn't Hide in the Crowd

*A large crowd followed and pressed around him.
And a woman was there who had been subject to bleeding for twelve
years. She had suffered a great deal under the care of many doctors
and had spent all she had, yet instead of getting better she grew
worse. When she heard about Jesus, she came up behind him in the
crowd and touched his cloak, because she thought, "If I just touch his
clothes, I will be healed." Immediately her bleeding stopped and she
felt in her body that she was freed from her suffering. . . .*

*"Daughter, your faith has healed you. Go in peace
and be freed from your suffering."*

MARK 5: 24-29, 34

· · · · · · · · · · · · · · · · · · ● ● ● ● · · · · · · · · · · · · · · · · · ·

THIS PERSISTENT WOMAN who pushed her way through the crowd toward Jesus remains nameless to us, but in many ways she represents so many who need Jesus' healing touch. She was one of the Lord's hidden ones: a case not to be publicly described because of its secret sorrow. She was a woman of few words and much shame. For years she had suffered from chronic bleeding that had drained away her life. Her body had slowly been sapped of its strength, and her very existence had become one of constant suffering and weakness.

Despite all she had suffered over the years, she was still *resolutely determined* to obtain health. So long as she had breath, she did not give up looking for a cure. She refused to resign herself to the inevitable until she had exhausted every effort to preserve her life and regain her health back. When at last she found the true Physician, she plunged into the thick of the crowd to touch Him by some means or other. If anything, she is to be admired for never, never giving up.

For twelve years she persevered in different ways and in the face of terrible agonies, suffering at the hands of many physicians. In those times, some of the methods used by supposed healers and charlatans were worse than the suffering itself. You think going to the dentist or having stitches today is an ordeal. The physicians of those days were a great deal more to be dreaded than even the worst diseases.

Yet the heroic woman of our text was a woman who endured every "medical" process that promised any hope to alleviate her suffering. And in the end, she had spent all her money trying to find a cure. Yet when all was said and done, she was no better but rather grew worse—and penniless.

To understand her suffering, which was much more than physical, you also have to understand the intense isolation she lived with every day. Her disease subjected her to grievous social penalties set forth in the Jewish ceremonial law. According to the Book of Leviticus (15:19-23), a woman with any issue of blood was considered ceremonially unclean. Imagine the shunning she had been subjected to for twelve years. That kind of constant rejection surely must have left emotional scars in her heart. How could it not have?

The specifics of the law of Moses were very clear and said that everything she sat on, and all who touched it, shared in the defilement. That public shame made her feel like an outcast under the ban of the law. In a way, she was no better off than the dreaded lepers who were shunned as well and banned from society. Hers was a lonely existence she lived. And no doubt it created great loneliness of spirit, which made her try to hide herself. Yet her venturing to approach Jesus speaks volumes of the seed of faith that was stirring in her heart.

Her *marvelous hopefulness* is to be admired. After all she had suffered, she still believed that she could be cured. She could have abandoned that hope long ago. Since no physician had been able to help her all those years, no one would have blamed her if she had thought her case was past hope. But no, she saw hope where others would have despaired and given up. Something within her spirit buoyed her up, and she still hoped for better days. So when she heard of Jesus, her heart leaped within her.

Though she was a woman of spirit, of resolution, and of hope, she also had a *vivid sense of her own unworthiness.* She was evidently afraid to face Jesus, lest He, knowing her unworthiness, as she knew and felt it, should spurn her and forbid her to approach Him. She was an unclean woman, and the shame of her disease prevented her from making any verbal request or open request. Though she would not approach Him face-to-face because of her sense of unworthiness, yet she believed in His divine power to heal.

News of Jesus' ability to heal was *spreading* fast throughout Palestine, and surely this woman had heard of all the wondrous cures He had already performed. She believed that the slightest contact with Christ would heal her. She resolved to trust in Jesus in sheer despair of doing anything else. What a grand faith was hers that made her rise above her weakness, overcome her depression of spirit, throw aside the lethargy that was creeping over her, and believe that everything would be different if she could but touch the hem of His garment. She no longer would have to deal with another pretender for healing who would fail her yet again. She sensed that within her grasp was One sent of God and clothed with infinite power who could heal even her incurable disease.

This woman's single eye of faith saw nothing but Jesus as she pushed her way through the crowd. With each step she took, her faith was rising, gathering strength the closer she got to Jesus. She would not be stopped until she touched Him! Oh that we would have the same singularity of faith as this poor woman. She knew that the power to heal was all *in Jesus,* and not in her, nor in her touch. No matter how despicable and unclean others might consider her, she pressed forward. She believed that Jesus could master every difficulty of her case, and that the result did not depend upon the mode of her touch, nor the length during which it lasted, but on Him alone.

And then the miraculous happens. She stretched forth her hand laden with the hope of faith. As soon as her fingers touched His garment, she was healed instantly. The grand success of her faith was seen when the Lord Himself stopped and asked who touched Him. The disciples wondered at His question with the crowd pressing in on Him from all sides. In fact, the context indicates that they thought His question was rather absurd. But Jesus instantly knew that power had gone out from Him.

Ignoring the disciples' comments, He looked around for the faith He had sensed with the touch. With the crowd around Him, many had touched Him, but this touch was totally different from all the others, and it pleased Him to the point that He had to discover its source. This touch had gone beyond the confines of what physical senses dictated as truth. This touch believed in His power over what her symptoms had told her for eighteen years. And so His blessed eyes looked around, and soon they rested upon a woman. Imagine the fears that probably ran through her. She was unclean and wasn't even supposed to be in public. Though she knew something wonderful had happened, she had no idea of how the crowd or the disciples would react. Yet as she gazed upon the eyes of Jesus, she did not feel so much alarmed as before. Afraid and trembling, the woman came and fell down before Jesus and told Him all the truth.

Then He gently raised her and said for all ears to hear, "Daughter, your faith has healed you. Go in peace and be freed from your suffering" (Mark 5:34). She now had the divine witness bearing witness with her spirit that she was indeed whole and healed and no longer an outcast to those around her. Touching Jesus not only healed her physically, it also lifted the social curse she had suffered under for all those years. She had received a double blessing that day from Jesus.

LIFE LESSON

· · · · · · · · · · · · · · · • ● ● ● ● • · · · · · · · · · · · · · · ·

Whatever disease of body or soul weighs you down, do not despair. Look away and fix your eyes on Jesus alone and exercise the courage that is born of desperation. Do as this woman did. Do not stop to consider your own unbelief, or answer your rising doubts and fears, or the warnings of others. But at once put out your finger, touch the hem of His garment in faith, and see what will come of it. Trust God the Holy Spirit to move you to cry out, "I will believe in His Word and trust my soul with Jesus." Do not go away until you have touched the Lord today by a believing prayer.

CHARLES SPURGEON

ALSO BY
LANCE WUBBELS

. . . . ● . . . .

A TIME FOR HEROES

September 11 was a day of unthinkable horror and destruction, but it became a day for American heroes. Heroes were everywhere you looked. Giants rose out of relative obscurity to cast long shadows across the smoke and dust and rubble. Ordinary American citizens suddenly caught in the crossfire of terrorism, put their lives on the line to preserve the lives of others.

In that sudden moment of time, the real heroes of our world stood out as brilliant luminaries cast against the darkest night. Most of them remain nameless to us, but their undaunted faces are engraved forever upon our hearts. This book is a tribute to their remarkable stories and a reminder of what true heroism and patriotism are.

ISBN: 0-7684-3046-1

For more information visit

. . . . ● . . . .

www.destinyimage.com
Available at your local Christian bookstore.